Just like Pamela, I had 20 jobs before I turned 23, so I loved her down-to-earth book. Pamela shares her life-changing experiences and heartfelt failures, offering a wealth of information in this smart book. There are no shortcuts to success, but Pamela will help you reach your personal success in a much shorter time.

BARBARA CORCORAN
Real Estate Mogul, Business Expert, and Shark Tank TV star

ONE CENT LEMONADE to MILLION DOLLAR DEALS

25 JOBS & 25 LESSONS I WISH I LEARNED SOONER!

PAMELA J. GOODWIN

DEDICATED

To my husband, **Eric**, and
my two wonderful sons, **Grant and Garrett**
– I love you more than words can be expressed!

ACKNOWLEDGEMENTS

As a book based on real life experiences, I have so many people to thank throughout the years...family, friendship, and professional life.

To all my family and friends who have always supported me for everything I always wanted to try and achieve in my life.

To my mom, *Sharon Zych*, who told me I could do anything I ever wanted to do in life and who sowed the seeds of my love for travel. You are truly the best mom in the world.

To my dad, *Ted Zych*, who taught me about business and taking chances and who passed away at the age of 58 from a massive stroke...and who is truly missed each day.

To my sister, *Lori Ortinau*, my brother-in-law, *Dr. Eric Ortinau*, my niece, *Megan*, and nephew, *Brett*: Best big sis ever; love traveling with our families together and visits to Chicago and Florida.

To my brother, *Scott Zych*, sister-in-law, *Amy*, nephew, *Tyler*, and niece, *Sara*: Best little bro anyone would ever want! Glad we live in the same neighborhood so we can have Sunday dinner cookouts together as a family!

To my life-long friends who I met in the seventh grade at St. Mary's Catholic School in Bellevue, Nebraska, and still best of buddies today—*Lynda Stangl, Julie Stangl, Jennifer Elman, Jennifer Icenogle, and Laura Wolfe*. We have shared so many adventures together through the years.

To my "business sisters"—*Linda Alexander*, we have shared many plane rides, dinners, and long conversations together; *Alice Zimmerman Seale*, for all of the "pep talks" we have each week and encouragement we give each other to keep striving for our dreams.

To *Rebecca Rivera*, one of my favorite bosses and mentors in the business and who took a chance and hired me and moved me to Baltimore, MD, so I could work for one of the best shopping center developers in the country.

To *Steve Dahm*, who decided to hire me full time and offered me an excellent job to relocate to Dallas, TX. You were such a generous boss who died too young from a heart attack at the age of 50.

To *Zig Ziglar, my favorite motivational speaker and author,* who I met in person and who told me I must write a book. Well, here I am writing and wish you were here to read it! "See You at the Top!"

To all my real estate and motivational mentors, *Barbara Corcoran, Robert Kiyosaki, and Tony Robbins,* who have all inspired me.

To all my family and friends in Nebraska. Go Cornhuskers! All of my friends in California and in Texas that have always supported me for my crazy adventures and next business ideas. You never know what I will be doing next!

CONTENTS

PROLOGUE

Life Is a Learning Game

Do you want to live a life less ordinary? Do you search your life and recognize the opportunities, seizing them when they come along? If not, why?

People who think **BIG** find opportunity the most, and people who trust their instincts take advantage of them.

Life is a learning game, my friend. Playing it safe is not good for your health or your future. Neither is listening to the people around you.

- How much have you managed to learn about yourself in your lifetime?

- What motivates you, drives you forward, and pushes you to succeed?

These are tough questions, but they need to be asked and answered.

Perhaps you have spent most of your life searching for your place in the world like I did. Maybe you were never meant to do one single thing with your life.

But let us not get ahead of ourselves; after all, this is just the beginning. And all good things have a decent start. This book is about helping you find yours.

It is a collection of things I have learned while working in more than 25 different jobs. I am pleased to say that despite all my challenges and "failures," *I have found success.*

One by one, these 25 amazing jobs have taught me the lessons I needed to learn in order to rise above my circumstances and become a financially and spiritually successful individual.

Through all my trials and experiences, I only had one simple thing on my side–*I loved to learn.* Not only did I play the learning game, but I played it to win. And win I did.

Of course, I only realized this much later on in my life. But that is why I am writing this book: to give you the lessons I learned in my life so that you can find a shortcut to success. *Let us begin.*

01

The Trailblazer Gene

· · · · · · · ·

"You Must Do The Things You Think You Cannot Do"

Eleanor Roosevelt

My motivation to succeed began at an early age. I was not the smartest, or strongest, or the most athletic, but I found a passion that was all my own–a passion for discovery, for life, and for learning.

But this would have all meant nothing if I was not raised to have guts–to show no fear when faced with change and evolution in my life. This is what saved me.

The Trailblazer Gene

I have had some pretty incredible women who have guided me in life, namely my great-grandmother, grandmother, and mother. I come from a long line of brave, determined women who have had the "trailblazer" gene.

Trailblazers feel like they can do anything because they trust their instincts. It is exciting and terrifying, and it is my strongest trait. I treasure it, as the women in my family have before me.

Three trailblazer women in my life: Great grandma, Grandma, and mom. Also in picture: my grandpa and dad
(Picture taken in June 1970)

First, I ask myself before making a change:

- *What is the **best** thing that could happen if I do this?*

- *What is the **worst** thing that could happen if I do this?*

As a little girl, my great-grandmother, Mildred Veslich, told me stories of her boat journey from Croatia to America. With so much at risk for her, I learned to see my life from a new perspective.

Make a list, side-by-side. If the worst possible thing that could happen is still better than your stagnant, boring situation – there is no reason not to go for it!

Great-grandmother Veslich   *Me and my great-grandmother*

With her story in my heart, everything always seemed so minor. She left her mother, father, and siblings at the age of 21 with her uncle in 1911, arriving in Ellis Island, New York, to start her dream life–her life of opportunity in America!

You may not know it yet, but you already have the opportunities that she left home to find.

The Ladies in My Family

I am grateful to my great-grandmother for teaching me a better life is always possible if you are willing to risk it all to get it. My great-grandmother taught me to always think and act like an immigrant–to make sacrifices in order to live a life of adventure, to become an explorer, to dream of a better life, and to seek new opportunities by taking risks. This drive to succeed started very early on for me.

When you have the guts to take **ACTION**, finding a life worth living becomes your ultimate goal. This is the legacy my great-grandmother, grandmother, and mother left me.

When I was a kid, my nickname was "Bugs," and it still suits me today because I cannot stay for too long in one place. My friends would joke with me that they would only put my address in pencil because I was always moving locations.

I grew up in Omaha, Nebraska, in the mid-60s in a middle class home. I am a "born in between" child and have had to overcome the Middle Child Syndrome and take on the positive characteristics of the middle child; we are more independent, think outside the box, feel less pressure to conform, and are great innovators and team leaders–like Bill Gates. I had lots of friends and loved sports, traveling, and being a tomboy. But I was not a great student; book learning was not for me.

Thank goodness for the positive influences in my life; they allowed me to see my self-image was not made up of what other people thought I could achieve.

But the world does not work that way. Things do not exist in a vacuum of black and white reasoning.

> *In this complex society, people will always try and box you in–put labels on you and reduce your wonderfully complex potential into "loser" or "winner."*

My mother had us try everything as kids to see what really interested us. We adventured in swimming, piano lessons, bowling, volleyball, soccer, basketball, softball, and acting classes. If we wanted to try it out, it was there to sample.

This in itself taught me how to see my life. How could other people define me, when I had not even found out who I was yet? That is the society that we live in!

My Grandmother's Career

When all the men in America had to be shipped off to war, the women worked in what were considered "male" jobs during World War II.

Back then, my grandmother, Frances Kubat, worked at Offutt Air Force Base in Bellevue, NE, at the Martin Bomber Plant. She was "Rosie the Riveter," the cultural icon that is still used in feminism today of women producing munitions and war supplies. Her job involved the prestigious task of riveting bolts in machine guns for precision movement. After the war was over, she worked in a meat packing company where she met my grandfather and then retired from Skinner Macaroni Company. I still remember as a young girl waiting on my grandparents' sofa and counting down 5,4,3,2,1 as grandma was being dropped off from work. To this day, I still buy Skinner product noodles in remembrance of my grandma. What a wonderful memory of a very hard working and inspiring woman in my life. When she died of ovarian and breast cancer, I learned an important lesson.

> *Nothing, and I mean nothing, is as important in your life as family and your health.*

If you have these two fundamentals, there is nothing you cannot achieve!

Grandmother, brother, great-grandmother, sister, mom, and me in 1967.

This is only the most important lesson anyone can ever learn in life, and if you learn it early, it makes everything easier.

- *There is more than one way to cook a goose! Your life does not have to be filled with one job, one direction, one goal. Part of the rich tapestry of our lives is that we get to spend 80+ years finding out what makes us happy.*

If, along the way, you find purpose and meaning among the chaos–great! But happiness does not exist in a vacuum. You cannot find it by standing still.

That is why I jumped from one job to the next. For me, there were 25 ways to cook a goose, and I am still cooking!

Self-Learned and Beyond!

My mother, Sharon Zych, was the first person in her entire family to graduate from college. She started when her three kids were in high school and did not stop until she had earned her Master's degree.

After working hard and spending 25 years of her life dedicated to civil service for the U.S. Government at Offutt Air Force Base, she is now retired with a great pension and health benefits.

It was she who helped teach me the value of supporting myself. Never let anyone support you, because they take away your ability to find out what you are really made of.

- From a very young age, I adjusted to a learning style that suited me best–the "hands on" type of learning they did not teach yet at school.

- I became very interested in earning money as a young child and was fascinated by different ideas, plans, and methods of making money.

- I did not know it yet, but thanks to the influence of the women in my family, I had learned to become *autodidactic*.

Autodidactism is a big word for a simple concept–a self-taught learner. When you have the ability to teach yourself, you are a natural autodidact.

The 1997 drama film *Good Will Hunting* follows the story of autodidact Will Hunting, played by Matt Damon. Hunting demonstrates his depth of knowledge throughout the film but especially to his therapist and in a heated discussion in a Harvard bar.

I am not talking about memorizing books or taking tests. Autodidactism is directed at many things depending on what interests you. For me, I became immersed in the pursuit of a better life.

The good news is that you can become (or realize that you are) an autodidact at any point in your life. Once you know this, you can harness it to make things better for yourself.

Foster a learning culture in your life. Learn from friends, family, teachers, experts, bloggers, and other notable authorities. The more ideas in your head, the better.

The Rabbit and the Hare: Who Wins?

I have always had this theory about the way most people live their lives. The theory is one I have already mentioned, but it warrants further explanation.

In my head, there are two types of people in this world. We are all the same, like rabbits and hares are, but with subtle differences.

You may recall the tortoise and the hare stories from Aesop's Fables growing up. In this story, the hare loses, and the tortoise, who takes things slow and steady, wins.

And really, this is a metaphor for what we are taught as children. Always be safe. Look left and right. Do not talk to strangers. Be scared of what life puts in front of you.

We are told through tales and stories that if we behave this way, things will turn out well for us. Of course, this is a horrible lesson to teach a child these days!

Back to my theory! Rabbits and hares both live, breed, and exist in the same space. So why do hares run free while rabbits are forced to live as pets in cages?

Simple. People that accept fear into their hearts as kids may not grow up to be brave enough to take the risks needed to become successful and find happiness.

The kids that grow up learning that there is more out there for them actively break out of the mold and try to find it. These are the wild hares that are happy and healthy in the field.

What is the moral of this story?

- Caged rabbits cannot win the race, because they choose to remain locked behind a prison of doubt, insecurity, and denial.

- Hares, on the other hand, can do anything. They have no limits because they discover things for themselves.

Are you a rabbit or a hare?

02

All Aboard:
Motivation Station

● ● ● ● · · ● ● ●

**"People often say that motivation
doesn't last. Well, neither
does bathing—that's why we
recommend it daily."**
Zig Ziglar

People have told me I am a lucky person. I have never considered myself lucky, because I have worked hard to be where I am today. As the saying goes, *"Luck is what happens when preparation meets opportunity."* I read a lot, I research a lot–I am always learning. This is because I am motivated to learn.

Motivation is almost always the one thing missing from the life of someone that is trying to become successful. If you can learn how to motivate yourself, it is a gift that will keep on giving.

When Life Gives You Lemons: Job #1

When I was four years old, I decided I needed to get a job. It was 1968, and I set up my very first cardboard lemonade stand, selling lemonade to the neighbors for one shiny penny. This was my very first experience earning money, and I find it is always the first experience that has the most lasting effect. *Can you remember yours?*

Back then I must have earned a whole quarter, and I was very pleased with this progress. I repeated it several times and learned more and more, even at that age.

My son and a friend of his recently manned a lemonade stand to raise money for recent tornado victims in Texas and Oklahoma. From my past experience as a kid, I suggested to them the location will make a difference where you set up, and do not put a price but take donations only. They listened, and in two hours they earned $352. How times have changed!

What did I learn from my first job?

- When life gives you lemons, make lemonade! Then sell it.

- If a four-year-old can make money, there is always money to be made.

- If something works well, it can always be improved to work better. Just look at my son using the same lemonade model to collect money for charity.

- To earn money you have to get up, have an idea, and then execute that idea. This requires motivation. Therefore motivation must be practiced daily to achieve big goals.

Watch What You Visualize...You Just Might Get It

I used to play a game as a child and imagined I lived in a beautiful stone castle, was married with kids, and drove a red Corvette. It was a great dream, but even then I knew the difference between dreams and real life.

Would a castle, marriage, kids, and a supercar make me happy? Probably not the material things (castle and car) but the other two yes! I learned early in life not to love anything that cannot love you back! Funny thing is we live in a neighborhood called Castle Hills, I am married with two children, and I drive a nice SUV. Motivation began for me in my imagination as I explored possibilities beyond what I was experiencing in my day-to-day life.

- Motivation is about visualization. Seriously, if you cannot see the end result in your mind, you will never take action to make it happen. Do you have a visualization board? I suggest cutting out pictures of what you want and creating a vision wall to look at every day.

- What gets you up in the morning? What is your reason for getting out of bed and pursuing a life outside of the dream world?

- For me, it was a combination of curiosity, the chance to grow, my kids, and that burning desire to find out what I am made of and what sort of life would suit me best.

I attended Catholic elementary and high school and had quite a few nuns as teachers. I was told early on I had a learning disability because I could not pronounce certain letters. This stigma lasted with me for a long time and created a low self-image. I was never book smart, but I had a lot of common sense.

Unfortunately, school was not for people like me; it was for above average and honor students. I was always placed in the lower classes. According to them, I was only an average student, but I never wanted to be just average.

- Being told "who" I was as a child motivated me to succeed more as an adult. I wanted to reach my goals, so I started working on them from an early age.

- Motivation comes from negative and positive places. Spot it, and then use it as fuel to drive you forward. Life will always give you good and bad opportunities. But all opportunities are a chance at extra motivation, even if you screw up!

The Competitive Edge: Pushing the Limits

When I was a child, I was naturally competitive, and I taught myself how to use competition to get ahead by playing lots of sports.

By the eighth grade, I had decided to try out for the boy's baseball team along with two of my friends, and you know what? We made it!

Back then girls playing on a boys' team was not something you saw every day–but we were good enough, and our risk paid off.

- Sometimes if you do not break the rules, you will not get the rewards. No girls would ever have tried out for the boys' team, but we did not care. We were as good as the boys and worked hard to make an impression. Hard work pays off.

- We learned to keep up and even outshine the boys on occasion. Even when I was standing waiting for the pitch and had the ball flying at my face–and I felt that we might be out of our league–we stuck with it. Reaching to be better makes you better.

- Stepping up your game is key to success. Being on the boys' baseball team taught me about being confident in my ability, and it built character. Just because people around you do not have faith in your abilities does not mean you are unable to prove them wrong by pushing the limits.

- Learn to play with anyone and take real chances! When I entered the job world, I realized how much being on a boys' team had taught me. Gender does not matter when you can keep up with the best; people respect that. It was a lesson I learned young, and it was an enormous help as I moved from job to job.

In every job in life, you need to be competitive and push the limits of what people expect from you. While it is not always possible to be the "best," you can still reach to be better and use that to earn the respect of people around you.

Setting Those Tasty Goals

I did not want to end up playing a supportive role in the life of a super star. *I always wanted to be the super star, the main event.*

- I identified that I wanted more from life and would therefore need to pursue it with more fury and vigor than most people had. At this stage, I did not know what I wanted, only that I wanted it.

- The next question was logical. What can I do about it? Easy! *Set goals.* I have been a firm believer in goals for as long as I can remember. Little goals lead to big goals, and big goals can change your life.

- What is preventing you from setting these goals? Obstacles always exist in life. If you are not moving forward willingly, there are things holding you back. Find out what they are, and set goals to eliminate them.

- Over the years I discovered there were always four reasons why I was not applying the motivation I felt.

   1. First of all, I was stuck in habits that did not allow me to change.
   2. Secondly, the goal was too lofty and the cost too high to achieve it.
   3. Next was means–could I even achieve the goal on my own?
   4. And finally, I was lying to myself about what I really wanted. These are pretty common things that hold you back.

- For example, if your goal is to lose weight and you have not been able to–why is that? Is it because you have not changed your habits? Is your goal too much to handle (losing 20 lbs in one month)? Can you afford healthy diet food and an exercise program right now? And do you really want to lose weight, or does the world just think you need to?

Motivation Is Like a Fridge...

So you see, motivation is not as simple as people think it is. It is actually very tricky and something that has to be applied to be used in your life.

I like to think motivation is like a fridge...

- *Planning:* When you start a diet, do you still go shopping for all the junk food you are not supposed to be eating? That is setting yourself up for failure. It is the same with motivation. If you do not remove the obstacles and fill your life with motivation, do not expect to find any when you open the fridge door.

- *Obstacles:* Imagine all the junk food in your fridge. Every night when you are warm in bed, you will be thinking about cheating just a little. In reality, you have already given yourself permission to fail. With motivation, if you do not remove the junk food (obstacles), they give you permission to remain unmotivated.

- *Exercises:* The next time you go shopping, streamline your list. Pick only the freshest organic veggies and lean meats. Put together a menu you love to eat, and make sure you have healthy snacks as well. With motivation, you need to add healthy exercises to your life that inspire you to be better. Without these daily tools and exercises, you will not remain motivated.

- *Long-Term Results:* If you keep filling your fridge with junk food, expect to keep gaining weight. But if you stop and instead **CHOOSE** to fill your fridge with healthy food, you will lose weight. In the same way, if you continue to motivate yourself, over time you will find your goals, hopes, and dreams are realized.

And that is why I believe motivation is exactly like a fridge. You can choose to use it wisely to support your goals, or you can fill it with rubbish and sabotage your chances of ever achieving anything.

It is down to choice—yours.

03

Fantastic on the Outside

● ● ● · · ● ●

"The definition of insanity is doing the same thing over and over and expecting different results."
Benjamin Franklin

There are different types of earning. Sometimes you can earn something with no effort; other times it takes enormous effort to achieve.

To get hired every single time I went to a job interview, I simply applied that logic. When you are fantastic on the outside and willing to earn a position in business, the world is completely open to you.

Chicken Is the New Pink: Job #2

The second job I ever had in the world was for working for my father. He took over the family poultry business from his father, and it happened to be South Omaha Poultry, a chicken distributor for local restaurants.

Sometime later I figured out selling colored live baby chickens and ducks around Easter time could be very lucrative. I was only eight years old at the time, but this great experience helped me to learn a very valuable lesson for life. You buy the baby chick for one penny, and you sell it for 50 cents. What a profit.

> *Everybody wants what everybody wants, and nobody wants what nobody wants.*

The cute little colored baby chickens and ducks sold incredibly fast, and no one else was selling them—just my family. Was it because we had a great product? Was it pitched at the right time? People were not rushing out to buy yellow chicks.

Me and my dad coloring "pink" baby chicks

- *There is always a new "pink." If you can make an idea popular, then you can sell it to everyone.*

- Later I applied this lesson to my ever-increasing interview skills. I needed to get jobs because I had to earn money. The only way to get the job I was interested in at that time was to become the "new pink."

- To get hired each and every time requires effort. It has to be earned. If you do the grunt work, you will never find yourself being passed over for a position. Just spray yourself pink in a room full of normal yellow chickens.

You are Always Selling Something

Thanks to my little pink chicken lesson, I soon became aware that–in the world of business–you are always selling something.

At the beginning of your career, you sell yourself. It is something you will have to do repeatedly if you are going to succeed. It is actually one of the more crucial life lessons in this book.

- *There is nothing wrong with selling yourself.* Businesses invest in human assets. Interviews are designed to establish whether or not you would be a good addition to their asset portfolio!

- *Remember my pink chicks?* They stood out because they were different. I am a firm believer in differentiating yourself from the "herd" by impressing your interviewers with your depth of knowledge.

- *Be memorable.* There are few things more memorable than a pink chick. If you are going to become that pink chick in an interview setting, you will need to understand the type of person you are up against. Research it well. Start off with finding a connection with the person interviewing you. People hire people they like!

- *Sell yourself with style.* Presentation and appearance are important in interviews. This sounds simple, but many interviewers decide whether they like you or not in the first few minutes of the meeting. Look great, and dress the part. Be sharp, be confident, but most of all do not be afraid to talk to them on their level–you are not a worker drone. Never be late! First impressions are key!

- *Know a lot about everything.* Be willing to talk at length about your resume, their business, your job, your skills, technical details, experience, and more. If you can let the interviewer know that you have a wealth of knowledge on your side, it is a tough thing to pass up. Remember to listen too.

- *Show and Tell.* Remember those days in school? It was always so much fun to bring something to school and tell about your item and then hearing the teacher talk. Right? Most people are visual people. It is more interesting to show some of your work, projects, spreadsheets, how you keep organized, etc. This will make you stand apart and be the pink chicken.

- *A little pink chick that walks around and around in circles is not going to be the first chick to sell.* Be very aware of your nonverbal cues in the interview. Often you communicate more about yourself with body language than you do while speaking.

When in Doubt...Learn It

I know how easy it is to be lazy. Laziness is glorified in modern society, and it is incredibly common–which is why it is okay to be lazy, right? I do not think so.

Like I said before, if you want to get noticed and **ALWAYS** get hired, then effort is your best friend. Together you can rule the world.

Invest time and effort into getting to know the industry and brand you are interested in. That way when you go to the interview, you will not be surprised by questions you do not understand. *Preparation is vital.*

- If you do not understand something or you have gaps in your knowledge, hit the books or the Internet. Learning and self-improvement are two key factors involved in the hiring process. Knowledge is the key to getting hired, but knowledge requires effort, understanding, and time.

- There is a good reason to go *above and beyond* when learning about a new industry for your next interview.

During the interview, you could get an opportunity to highlight the knowledge that you have for the benefit of the business. This will impress the interviewer and result in a call back.

- Specifics matter. It is nice that you have prepared for the basic things that interviewers ask, but what about the specific things? Winging it in this competitive world is not going to get you anywhere. If a pink chick is up against a blue chick, the one that sells will be the one with the most "know-how."

This is how I managed to integrate myself into 25 different job choices. I was never shy, and I always tried to be the pink chick. Like it or not, businesses want the best people, and the best people are very rarely just like everyone else.

Focus on the Details

You are always selling something, and there are many parts involved when you try to sell yourself at a job interview. Getting hired right away is not easy.

However, you should focus on the details…

- Most people get the small details of the job application process wrong. This immediately eliminates their chances at getting hired. If you can get these basic details right every single time, there is nothing stopping you from being the pink chick.

- Research what should and should not be in a professional resume. If you can afford it or you have the skill, make sure that your resume is 100% professional. That means no spelling errors, no formatting problems, and no outdated cover letters.

- Always streamline your resume for the job you want. Do NOT hand in a standard resume at every single job you want. Interviewers can see in a second if you are really interested in the position or if you are simply sending out bulk job applications.

- Keep it short and current, and EDIT the parts that are not relevant. Whenever I applied for a new job, I only listed the jobs I had done in the past that would contribute to getting me an interview. If I had told them I had been in 25 different positions, I would never have been hired.

- Write a unique and personalized cover letter. If you can find out the name of the interviewer beforehand, include it in your letter. The extra effort is what makes all the difference to an interviewer has seen 100 bad examples of a resume.

- When you go for your interview, be mindful of your attitude. Interviewers are not only chatting to you about your skills, but they want to see if you will fit in with the business culture and social dynamics of the workplace. Always smile and be friendly, and do not let your personal life or moods ruin your interviews.

Why Innovation Beats Boring

Let us be honest—why buy a boring yellow chick when you can buy a special pink Easter chick! The two are essentially the same, but one always comes out on top.

Innovation is a very important part of business, and it can give you the edge in a job interview. Believe me, innovation beats boring every time.

- Find solutions for the interviewer. A person who has solutions has ideas. They may not be particularly good ideas or great solutions, but having them is the point. Too many people are content with clicking along doing the bare minimum and having no ideas at all.

- When you hire a "pink chick" instead of a normal yellow one, you are making it very clear that you want innovation to be part of your business. Innovation is all about ideas and NOT being part of the problem. If a business is looking for new hires, it often means they want to introduce new ideas and innovation into the business.

- In an interview environment, the candidate who looks great, speaks well, and has a lot of decent ideas will always be the most viable option. You do not have to be the best; you just have to be the most memorable, dynamic, and innovative. Push ideas, a great attitude, and appearance, and you will always win.

- Finally, find the one thing that makes you **UNIQUE**. What is your unique selling point? All products have one, and you need one as well. The stronger your selling point, the higher your *value*. It is how people get promoted. And in business, *knowledge is just about the strongest selling point you can have.* Begin strong and get hired!

If you apply these little lessons in your next interview, you will get hired. The pink chick lesson has never let me down. Do your research, become an asset before they have even hired you–and they will not be able to say no.

04

Footsteps and Faces

● ● ● · · ● ●

"Everything passes and vanishes; everything leaves its trace; and often you see in a footstep, what you could not see in a face."
William Allingham

Iknew from a very young age that I wanted to have a lot of money–and be very famous. Looking back, I can see now that what I really wanted was respect. I wanted people to remember me–to be important enough to be remembered.

It was my father who taught me that in order to be memorable, you have to take action. Footsteps make a person memorable, not faces.

Yes They're Alive! Job #3

The third job I was given happened to be at the same place I managed to source those popular chicks and ducklings that I was selling. Being an eight-year-old entrepreneur, I found it necessary to gain some real work experience from my father.

Still at South Omaha Poultry, my father began teaching me about the ins and outs of running a business. I was very enthusiastic and eager to make money.

It was hard work to own a poultry business in the '70s and not much competition. Who wants to deal with cold dead chickens in a cold freezer every day? I learned that you have to be the best in your industry and a few other things my dad taught me.

- **Be different.** Not many kids got to grow up around livestock. Instead of avoiding it, I embraced it and used it to my advantage.

- **Do something unusual.** During the holidays my dad's company was the place to pick up the freshest poultry in town for that special family dinner.

My dad - Ted Zych (taken in 1996)

It Is Not about Who You Are...

The days at my father's poultry business were long and educational. An eight-year-old with an entrepreneurship complex was practically in business heaven. The thing that stuck with me was the way everyone at the company treated my dad. He had respect from everyone–his workers who worked with him for many years, his managers, his suppliers, but most of all his customers. When I asked him about it, he said, "It is not about who you are; it is about the impression you leave behind."

- Anyone in any career can have respect and be memorable. Being memorable is not about having the flashiest car, the most money, or the largest, most dangly diamond earrings. Respect is earned. But you need to actively show people that you are a person of integrity and someone to be respected.

- These days customers only know you via telephone calls, brief meetings, emails, texts, and chat messages. They have a limited perspective on who you are. To make an impression, do something impressive! Be exceptional!

- My father always *under promised and over delivered*. It was his way of differentiating himself from his competition. The impression was not lost on his customers, who were very loyal to him. I stand by that motto to this day.

- Being memorable is not about looking different or even feeling different. People do not see you when you are like everyone else. They only see you when you DO something worth noticing.

Having an opinion is nice but not memorable. Having an experience is far more dynamic. That is why DOING is far more valuable than seeing. Talking about a mountain is great, but having climbed that mountain and conquered it is far more impressive. Do not forget to DO to fuel the respect that people have for you.

My father was memorable to his customers because he always made very sure that they got perfect service and a little extra, just because. For customers who were used to having problems with their poultry partners, it made him stand out.

Thinking Ahead and Beyond

What makes you stand out? When I was a child, my parents' friends always remembered me as the one that wore mismatched clothing.

It was only much later on in life that I realized to think ahead is to get ahead. Applying fresh perspectives to any problem–and finding solutions to potential future problems–was a big part of my father's job. It is a big part of any job if you want to be successful.

- The past is where all of your mistakes live. Focusing on the past is a surefire way to undo the success you may have in the future. You should always be looking ahead, not behind. That is how you keep progress trundling on.

- When you are feeling low, all you need is one fresh thought about the future. You will be surprised by what you can achieve when you are consciously looking out for negative behaviors you have practiced in the past.

- Being memorable is about always being able to look

ahead. We all experience difficulties from time to time. The trick is to see them for what they are–passing moments in time. Do not allow these passing moments to define who you are.

- Thinking ahead means planning to become the person you were meant to be. For me, that meant getting out of my own way. I knew the average job would not hold my interest when I left college, so I actively pursued interesting careers.

- I learned from my father that it is important to set a good example, to be authentic, and to really listen when people talk to you. Most people do not listen; they are just waiting for their turn to speak. He differentiated himself from people like that by being ethically on point, by caring about his work, and by focusing on customer relationships.

The Experience Formula

Experience is the most direct route to success in all aspects of life: work, home, relationships, and family. But it is not only your experience that matters. In fact, experience can make you "fit in" more than it can make you "stand out."

That is why to continue to become a memorable person you will have to inspect what you expect! All success in life depends on your experience and the experience that other people have when they work with you.

Before you work with others, you need to consider what to expect from them and if they are able to achieve this level of expectation. I have been surprised to discover on more than one occasion that my perspectives about people have been distorted.

- Align your expectations with the capabilities of the people that you are working with. Make sure that you do the same with yourself to prevent customer disappointment.

- To be memorable, you must first be clear. Communicate your expectations clearly with the people around you. Do not simply assume that they are on the same page. My father went to great lengths to make sure that everyone knew their role.

- You will find that the people who are able to monitor and manage their performance best are the ones that tend to stick in your mind. Never underestimate the power of doing things properly, because most people do not make it that far.

- Experience is only valuable to an individual if it allows them to get ahead or to rise above their position. The more experience you gain, the more ammunition you will have to become a memorable person.

- There are thousands of reasons to be like everyone else, and it is the easier option. It takes great effort to stand out and to be the person who other people want to deal with. Only experience will show you where you need to improve to get this right.

Be Your Own Personal Brand

If you want to leave some powerful footsteps behind when you work with people, you will need to become your own personal brand. When you think of yourself as a brand, there are a lot of basic changes you can make to become more memorable.

My grandfather was the man who first started our poultry business. Back then, we were at war, so food was rationed and times were tough. Grandpa would give people chickens, and people loved him for it. It made him a local hero.

He allowed struggling folks to pay when they could afford it. They would bring the chickens to him to be killed and cleaned. Not only did this stimulate his business, but it made him an important part of the community. Now that is a personal brand!

- *Accept who you are.* Know what makes you unique and different. Everyone has a job, kids, a car, a house, and a hobby. What sets you apart? Define your top three attributes, and use them in communication to show people who you are.

- *Always look the part.* If you want respect and you have a version of yourself in your mind that impresses other people, dress like that person. Sharp clothes and looking well turned-out is a skill and lets other people know you have a purpose.

- *Be consistent.* There is no point being highly memorable one day then blending into the shadows every day after that. If you want to be remembered, you need to constantly work at it. Make people notice you.

- *There is good memorable and bad memorable.* You want yours to the positive kind that leaves behind a solid, clear, and lasting impression based on your experiences with the people you are targeting.

In the real world, a brand logo stands for quality, consistency, and innovation. You need to begin to think of yourself as a brand so that you can market yourself accordingly.

> *Do not be afraid to show people your best. It will already make you more memorable than most.*

05

Hello? Yes.
This Is Life Calling

● ● ● · · ● ● ●

"Don't reserve your best behavior for special occasions. You can't have two sets of manners, two social codes— one for those you admire and want to impress, another for those whom you consider unimportant. You must be the same to all people."

Lillian Eichler Watson

This is the technology age, and you live in it. But sometimes new technologies can result in the loss of a personal connection–the kind you need to succeed in business. I find this most often with phones.

People these days have terrible phone etiquette, if you can even get them on the phone! Emails, texts, Skype, and instant message systems do not make it all right for you to have a terrible presence when you are chatting on your mobile.

Nothing Sucked Quite as Hard: Job #4

Once I had spent enough time working with my dad and had a firm grasp of what happened over there, I decided to get a "real" job. That job was selling Hoover vacuum cleaners by cold calling prospects and being a much-hated telemarketer.

I quickly learned that people were not happy to get calls from someone they did not know–especially if that person was after their hard-earned money. From this job, I developed a hatred for talking to people on the phone.

I only discovered years later that phone etiquette was a powerful business and social tool and that having the right temperament on a call was a real asset.

- What do you say to people between hello and goodbye? Your voice is part of your personal brand, so a phone conversation is an opportunity to extend the value of that brand to your customers, friends, and family.

- I learned that people want to be heard. They do not want a pitch. They want to have their concerns dealt with first. Once you have alleviated their fears and concerns, then you can talk business…or sell them something.

Contact: Launch Ship

I must say, working as a cold caller was rough, and I was quite young to be doing it. But I learned that the way you contact people influences their decisions about you. If you want to sell something or do business, you have to think of your calls as "first contact."

Imagine how you would communicate if you landed on an alien world, with alien inhabitants–and you needed them to fix your broken ship. How would you make first contact?

- You would introduce yourself and provide some background knowledge. You cannot expect anyone to care about who you are if you do not tell them. You have contacted them, and it is your responsibility.

- When you talk to them in the future you will use a standard, yet professional, greeting that they will recognize as a friendly, open invitation to communicate.

- Offer your name in your greeting so that they will remember it. It also makes the call more personal when you are speaking to a person and not just a disembodied voice.

- Naturally, the aliens will be suspicious of your motives. It is up to you to allay their fears and let them know that you do not mean to cause them any harm. In business calls, the same logic applies. Get to the "why" you are calling as soon as you can.

- Once you have made first contact, it is your job to maintain a pleasant and professional relationship with the aliens so that you can gently persuade them to help you fix your ship. If you want to do business with someone, calling is a great way to keep the relationship alive and moving forward.

- Aliens can get restless. Try not to put anyone on hold, as it can frustrate people. The last thing you want is a frustrated potential customer.

If you continue to be professional, direct, and friendly, eventually you will be able to launch your ship off the planet. Phone etiquette is directly responsible for new business, repeat business, and maintaining quality relationships with the right people.

This Is Your Trump Card

You may not know it yet, but being great on the phone is a serious trump card these days. So many people dislike talking on the phone, and with all the technology alternatives, they do not have to do it as often anymore.

But this leaves a gap wide open for the more personal form of communication–calling. When you are genuinely great on the phone, it can be a major asset to your business.

- Do not be afraid to call people. **A voice is worth a thousand emails!** In business, if your phone is not ringing off the hook, you are not using it properly. That is because your customers should WANT to call you because it is so easy and helpful.

- Donald Trump is famous for saying that if your email is longer than 10 words, you should pick up a phone. This is how he built his empire, and modeling your own efforts after successful people is a great life strategy.

- Make it easy for people to contact you whenever they want to. Have office hours, but be available to talk whenever your customer needs to–especially if they are involved in the buying process.

- Practice being respectful of those around you by maintaining a private conversation on the phone without shouting in public. People who shout in calls are hard to like, and that is never good for sales.

Calling your customers with a fantastic phone temperament is one trump card that will serve you well in every aspect of any business venture. There is nothing nicer than talking to a friendly, helpful person on the phone.

I bet you have been called by a cold caller who was very good at the job. I bet you stayed on the phone a little longer with them because they were respectful, energetic, and interesting. If they can achieve success, it should be that much easier for you when dealing with actual clients and partners.

What Is Your Voice Picture?

Your voice creates a mental image in the mind of the person that you are speaking to. They automatically imagine where you are and what you are doing when they first hear your voice.

What sort of voice picture do you illustrate for your customers?

A voice is a powerful tool; it can be just as emotional as a face.

- *Be aware of the tone of your voice and that your feelings affect your phone temperament.* Do not call customers if you are frustrated, irritated, angry, sad, or rushed. They will hear the emotion in your voice and wonder if they are the cause of it. You can alienate customers by doing this.

- *Be aware of the language that you use.* The words that you choose when speaking with a customer can really affect the meaning of what you are trying to say. "I just wanted to quickly let you know about x," is very different from "I am calling about the x property that you wanted to hear about." Words matter!

- *Pronouncement and accents are important.* If you have a regional accent or a foreign accent, make sure that you enunciate every word and speak slowly enough so that even a distracted listener would be able to understand you.

- *Imagine your voice as a painting.* When you call customers, you want to create clean, even lines with pleasant colors and vibrant subjects. If you call them full of emotion, then instead of a calming, motivational painting, you will get a torrid squall of confused brushstrokes. Do not allow your voice to become abstract art.

You see, your voice picture is a very important part of proper telephone etiquette. Before I answer the phone–no matter what is happening–I take three deep breaths, calm myself, and then answer. And I always make sure that my listener **has my full attention.**

To Listen or Not to Listen

As I mentioned earlier, there is a very clear distinction between listening and not listening. When you listen to a customer, you can pick up on subtle voice clues that can help you during the selling process.

If you hear nervousness, you can alleviate it. If you hear fear, you can be supportive and ease their fears. Listening is the most difficult skill to learn as a telephone master.

In business, the ability to anticipate the emotions of your customers is a real asset. If you can gauge how they feel, you can think ahead, strategize, and improve your sales rates.

- The length of a call matters. Set a time when talking with someone on the phone. A good 15 minutes is enough for most people to communicate what they need to say. Time is a valuable commodity, and you should spend it wisely.

- When you set the length of your calls, you eliminate what I like to call "client abuse," which is really just a clingy client who spends an hour with you on the phone when that is not particularly necessary. These can be time-wasters.

- Have standards. There may be times when a client becomes upset with you or disgruntled. Have a process ready for dealing with angry phone clients. Diffuse the situation instead of making it worse by ending up in a shouting match. It happens.

- Always, always, always hear what they are trying to say before adding in your piece. You know what you want to say. Your goal in a phone call is to evaluate what the intentions of the other caller are.

This is not a Shakespearean play. There is no question when it comes to listening. If you are going to be a big player, then you need a big telephone game. This "old" technology is still the most efficient way to communicate with people in business.

> *As talk show host Larry King says, "I never learned anything when I was talking."*

06

Manners Matter

● ● · · · ● ●

"Your career success in the workplace of today–independent of technical expertise–depends on the quality of your people skills."

Max Messmer Jr.

I was always told to mind my manners and respect my elders when I was growing up. But how do you go from being well-behaved to being well-liked?

These days being a "people person" is a skill that will take you all the way to success. Everything is "social business this" and "social communication that." Does being a people person give you an edge over other people?

It's Crying, but It's Clean: Job #5

My fifth job was not a glamorous one. I decided to earn some extra money by babysitting kids for people in our neighborhood. I will never forget that feeling the first time I had to look after someone's baby.

Looking back, I was far too young to be doing that. Even though I had an entrepreneurial spirit, the baby might as well have been an MIT engineered baby-robot for all I knew about it.

I charged a whole 50 cents an hour and was a very popular choice for parents where I lived. Even though I had zero experience, I had something better–people skills!

- I treated adults like I treated my own parents, with respect. I kept them informed about what I intended to do with their kids and how I would keep them entertained.

- Instead of watching television when the baby was sleeping, I would clean their house. That way, when they arrived back from being out, they walked into a nice, sparkly-clean home. It was an added extra at no cost that made me the number one babysitter in our area.

I learned how to be responsible while doing this job, not just for the kids I was looking after, but for myself and my "clients." Parents with babies are permanently exhausted. When you throw in a free clean, they become your customer for life!

The Trust Equation

Without interpersonal skills, you should not expect people around you to trust you very much. If you are bad at communicating with your customers, they will be reluctant to trust you.

In every business relationship, there is a trust equation. The equation itself is made up of different variables, namely communication skills, people skills, work ethic, and the cost to service delivery balance.

Having strong interpersonal skills begins with trust. If people do not trust you, they will not keep you as a partner for very long. That is just how business works.

- *Commitment matters.* To build trust, you must be committed to providing your client with the ultimate service. ***Go the extra mile.*** Blow their minds! I did not have to clean the house, but I knew it would guarantee me a repeat babysitting position.

- *Always be upfront and honest.* If you say you are going to do something, do it. And use some extra effort to prove to your clients that you have done it. Cleaning the house was evidence enough for parents that I was not a lazy, irresponsible sitter.

- *Consistency is key.* To gain trust, be consistent. It is really easy, but most people are lazy and will not make the effort. Whenever I babysat, I cleaned; it was my "something special." If I only did it occasionally, many of my parents would have been disappointed. It was an unofficial service that was very popular.

- *Show how much you care.* It is rare that business people care about other business people. But when you show your clients that you truly care, the response will be worth it. I allowed tired parents a night of rest and recovery. This was worth more to them than the measly 50 cents an hour I charged. They loved me!

- *Credibility is the final piece of the puzzle.* When news began to spread about my "special extra," I was never out of babysitting work. Eventually I had enough parents bashing down my doors that no one ever questioned my credibility. The proof was in the client satisfaction.

Age Is but a Number, Dearie

I am a believer in constant learning, so age did not really matter to me. If I felt like I could achieve something, I went and did it–despite my age.

A dance class instructor I once had told me that I could create a better attitude just by changing my shoes. You walk a lot different if you have on high heels vs. flip flops or cowboy boots vs. tennis shoes. Wear your best shoes to boost your attitude and confidence. And he was right.

Perception, attitude, trust, and credibility–these are all factors that motivate the relationships that you have with other people. If you are going to be an effective people person, then you need to brush up on these skills!

- *You can talk to anyone, at any time in your life, with respect and candor.* I spoke with adults like they were my peers from a very young age. The trick is to treat everyone you come across with kindness, compassion, and respect.

- *Perception is the root of all evil.* Within three seconds of meeting you, someone has already made their mind up about you. Give them something positive to think about. Be well-dressed and clean, speak well, and be polite yet assertive. That is all it takes.

- *Attitude can affect relationships.* You may not realize it, but you have an attitude towards different things in life. When I babysat, I consciously adopted a positive attitude and projected my exceptional work ethic in everything I did. Be aware that you are always projecting something. If it is not a choice, it is a side effect.

- *Trust and credibility are the cornerstones of having great people skills.* It does not matter how old you are; if people believe you and trust you, they will give you work. It is your job to be believable and trustworthy in business.

At a young age, I managed to convince parents that I was the best option for them. I was not as old as other babysitters, and I did not have medical training or basic child caring skills. What I did have was something better–the ability to make myself indispensable to tired parents. People skills that are properly honed can do this for you.

The Everything and Nothing Conundrum

It is great fun to be a people person. But the first time you encounter a client who does not like you–just because–well, that can be a hard lesson to learn. I will never forget the first time it happened to me.

I was babysitting for a family, and the boy recently had his cast removed from his leg. Well, you guessed it–he stood up and fell and could not get up. I did not know what to do except run to my friend's house across the street since her mom was a nurse to get her to help me. I remember when the mom returned home she was not very happy with me. This ended my babysitting career at that home.

When I went home crying, my mother told me that some people will never be impressed with you, like you, or care about you. As she said, **"You can't be everything to everyone, or you will be nothing to no one."**

- People are easily defeated by obstacles such as these. They believe that because some of their clients are never happy, they should not bother trying to impress the other clients they have. That is nonsense!

- If there is one thing you can bank on in this life, it is that there will be people that you have to deal with that will not like you. For whatever reason, they will not appreciate your service or the fact that you go the extra mile for them. It happens a lot.

- Having people skills means being able to determine who will appreciate your effort and who will never be satisfied. Personally, I find that the less I do business with people who do not appreciate me, the happier I am. You can choose your clients.

Your job is to focus your people skills on the RIGHT people. As you progress in your career, you will see what I mean. The important part is that you never stop trying.

Fostering a "Just Because" Attitude

You may think doing all of that extra work cleaning my clients' houses was not worth my time–but think again. I had a goal: to impress my clients so they would hire me again. Using this extra bit of thoughtful work, I achieved that goal nearly every time.

It was my father who helped me develop a "just because" attitude. When a family member goes down to the shop and returns home with something special just for you–even though you did not ask for it–it is that feeling that makes clients love you.

You want to make them feel ultra-special, and a "just because" attitude does that. Why clean their house? Just because, that is why! Your clients do not have to know that it is part of a strategic plan. All they need to know is that you gave them a high value, low cost service.

- Put yourself in the ruby red slippers of your ideal client. It is your choice to give them either a wicked witch experience or be the hero of the day. If you would be blown away by the extra service, then chances are they will be. Think Nordstrom's department store!

- I learned if you are the only one doing something different, you have an edge on your competition. It became a big deal to have me babysit your kids because none of the other sitters wanted to clean for free.

- If a client seems suspicious of your extra services, let them know that you value them as a customer and expect nothing from them. You will go above and beyond "just because" that is your ideal way to nurture repeat business.

If I could become a super babysitter with zero experience and only people skills, then you can do the same thing in your career. The formula works, and I have never stopped using it. And you know what? Most of my clients really appreciate me.

07

Juicy Grade
An Experience

● ● • • • ● ●

"Do you know the difference
between education and experience?
Education is when you read the fine
print; experience is what you get
when you don't."

Pete Seeger

I once read the best way to learn about having a successful business is to start one. It makes sense, but realistically, it is high risk trying to do something you have never done before. It can end in a bit of a debacle.

Instead, I learned if you want to be the best at something, you should learn FROM the best. And this can be applied in business with very successful results.

Breaking News and Windows: Job #6

Job number six was an exercise in learning for me. Many of the most wealthy and successful people in the world started with a newspaper route (Warren Buffett, Walt Disney, Tom Cruise, Martin Luther King, Jr., Wayne Gretzky, Bob Hope, Jackie Robinson, John Wayne, and President Dwight D. Eisenhower). So I had to have one.

I began delivering newspapers to everyone in my area. The *Bellevue Leader* and the *Omaha World Herald* were my two products. I made one cent per paper that I dropped off.

I also made tips by collecting the dues for the *Omaha World Herald*. Truth be told, I made a lot more money getting tips from readers than I ever did delivering the papers.

- If you want to learn from the best, you should try to experience what they have experienced. Having a paper route taught me the value of "getting out there" in order to make decent money.

- In every job opportunity, there are avenues that you can identify that will make you more money. With newspaper delivery, it was not long before I realized that the money was not in the delivery but in the people I was delivering to.

- This taught me a valuable life lesson about service delivery–that even though your work should always be good and delivered on time, you need to focus on the relationship with the customer if you want to leverage the earning potential.

And the Runner Up Is...

Have you ever watched those Miss America pageants on television with your family? My favorite part is when they announce the first runner up.

The first runner up almost won but did not quite make it. Their only reaction is to suppress an overwhelming sense of disappointment while still trying to maintain some dignity and decorum on stage.

You never hear from these people again, while the winner goes on to be a humanitarian, business person, and public figure. Is the difference between the runner up and Miss America so great? Nope. But there can only be one winner.

- *It is important to learn about action and follow through in business.* Taking action is crucial, but most people do not let it play out to the end. Instead, they shrink back into the shadows like a runner up at a beauty pageant.

- *Choose specifically where you want to work. They must be the best.* Aim high; they will be the ones that train you. When you work for the best in the industry, you become the best.

- *Once you have learned all you can about the ins and outs of your job, you are now free to ascend or to quit and start your own company.* Working for the best is like getting a crash course in success.

- *Create a bucket list from a young age.* Set yourself some lofty goals and work towards them. Life is about continuous training, so you might as well choose where you want to study!

- *Create lists and use them to inch closer to your goals.* Anything is achievable if you have a step-by-step process to get there. Instead of setting goals to lose 30 pounds, set micro-goals to lose one pound at a time. Record everything for later review.

Words in Sales

Being in the newspaper business, even in the bike delivery side of things, showed me how much people value the appropriate use of words used in the right context. Newspapers did not have any mystery; they were filled with news.

Sales and marketing were once simple concepts, but now–with the Internet and social media–the world has changed. Words are so much more valuable now. That is why learning how to use them accurately while you are training at your 9–5 is essential.

- Take notice of how the people around you communicate with their clients. When you notice something special, jot it down. I would suggest keeping a success training journal for when you are working for the best in the biz.

- Detail how the company structures their text content for marketing materials, client emails, online marketing, newspaper ads, memos, staff meeting minutes; wherever words are used, study them. They will make you a better business person.

- Recognize we are transitioning from a siloed sales experience to a social sales experience, where engaging with your clients directly on public platforms is now the preferred method of promotion and endorsement.

- Words make sales happen. Measure yours! Stay away from the old hyped up language of the nineties; no more "expert, best in class, high ROI, low hanging fruit, value added, turn-key solution" jargon that has been used to death.

- Instead, allow your customers words to speak for you. Focus on learning how your 9–5 company gets positive feedback from customers using the various promotional platforms out there, then do it for yourself.

Words have more power when they are sincere, so be intentional with every piece of content that you use in your business. Do not allow bad word choices to tarnish your reputation. A business with great content is a business worth trusting.

Being a Work Politician

I knew I had to get a good job to be financially stable, but I did not know what sort of job to get.

I eventually figured out that jobs are so much more than just "work." If I could earn lots of tips delivering newspapers when I was a child, then I could turn any job into a high earner.

I like to call this being a "work politician." Politicians are very diplomatic in their dealings; they make sure the maximum amount of people like them according to a strict set of predefined agendas. It makes choosing your next job a little easier.

- Even if you do not know what you want to do or be, think like a work politician. They would never stay in a place that does not pay them enough and does not teach them anything new. The whole point of work is to learn and grow.

- As a work politician, spend time developing the core business skills that will make you president one day.

To get to the top, politicians know a lot of influential people; they have a broad network they can access. Make connections at every position.

- Knowledge is the key to becoming president one day. But you cannot do it alone. On your journey, identify people that you would like to work with one day. Profile your ideal work colleague.

- A work politician is not interested in working hard. They work smart. They get the most return for the least effort. That way when they put in a lot of effort, they get significant returns.

If you want to be president of your own company one day, you will learn from the best just like a politician does. Stay balanced, be amiable, and make connections. Never burn bridges, and be sure to take calculated risks. Always pursue higher learning opportunities.

Efficiency Wins the Day

I wish someone had told me the only way to learn how to be a good "business person" is to train with the best. And I wish someone had told me ALL work is training.

Of all the jobs I did over the years, I learned the most efficient businesses were also the most successful ones. Businesses that do well do not "wing it"; they are brimming with procedures, systems, and plans.

- There is a difference between being loyal to a company that you work for and suffering for the good of your company. No person should ever work at their own expense, or resentment will move into the cubicle across from them.

- Never put the company first. Companies are not people. They are designed to be efficient, even if it means demanding unrealistic amounts of work from you. A drone says, "Yes," and then works themselves to death. A leader says, "No, I am not willing to sacrifice my health and happiness for my job."

- Do not confuse effort with results. The best businesses only care about results. You should have a vision that you add to each day. How are you moving forward? What are you learning? Are you getting better or worse and why?

- When you work for the best, you also have to take on a lot of stress because they will not accept mediocre work. Keep in mind that they can walk you out at any time, and then what have you got? You are your own asset. Learn, then move on.

Efficiency really does win the day in business. But it can be a very long and complex process learning how to be efficient on the same level as the best businesses in the world. With time, you will train yourself to be an efficient business person—keep this in mind.

08

Are You Always on Sale?

• • • · · • • •

"Your self-worth has nothing
to do with your craft or calling,
and everything to do with how
you treat yourself."

Kris Carr

Sometimes you are your own worst enemy in business. Lack of knowledge will get you every time. But some lessons have to be learned to be absorbed.

How much do you think you are worth right now? Write it down. How much do you earn? Write it down. I bet that you believe you are worth a lot more than what you earn.

A Corny Morning Situation: Job #7

My seventh job was grueling, dirty, buggy, and sweaty–everything I am pleased to say that I do not enjoy about a job. Every morning at 5 a.m. I would get up to de-tassel corn in the Iowa cornfields.

De-tasseling corn paid extremely well, but boy, was it a horrible job. That was not a bad thing though; it taught me a valuable lesson.

- You need to calculate your worth. If you do not do this, you will never know if your work-to-payment ratio is acceptable.

- The days were hotter than being wrapped in a thermal sleeping bag and tied to a camel that has been set loose in an African desert. I hated every moment. But the money was so good! What was I to do? Calculate my worth of course.

- After taking all the factors into consideration, I decided the money was not equal to the amount of hatred I was progressively feeling towards the work. That was the day I figured out that I was not into manual labor.

You have to assess your worth right now. If you slave away and do not get paid enough, or if the work is too hard and makes you miserable, you have to consider your main asset– you. The big lesson learned here was that **no amount of money can make you love a job that you hate.**

You Tell People How to Treat You

Have you ever wondered how some interns are promoted at the same time yet earn two completely different salaries? It all comes down to self-worth. The truth is that you teach people how to treat you.

If intern one has a higher self-worth than the other, the same scenario will play out two completely different ways.

- Both interns are offered full-time employment at $2,500 a month, with limited benefits. They will have to be willing to work extra hours and on weekends. It is a competitive job, and both people are pleased with the offer.

- Intern one is confident. She asks for $2,800 a month, with full benefits. She also requests they pay her overtime. If they cannot pay her overtime, then she would like a salary of $3,500 to cover her time. She is willing to work weekends and extra hours if the company pays her for her time. The company agrees.

- Intern one is not confident. He agrees to the $2,500 with limited benefits. He agrees to working overtime for no pay. As a result, he is worked far more than intern one, who is paid more and works less. Who is better off in this scenario?

So you see, you tell people how to treat you. Assume that you are your own company–a one person company–even when you are working for someone else. They do not own you. They cannot make demands on you. They need you.

Ignore the market. You are not other people. What you bring to the table, only you can bring, and good managers will see that. There is a risk that they will refuse. If they do, renegotiate or leave. If they will not pay you what you are worth now, they never will.

Putting Cash Dollars in Your Pocket

Money is the reason why you work. It has always surprised me how some people treat their jobs like they are all-important.

There needs to be an appropriate cash-to-time trade off. You sell your company your expertise and time in exchange for money. Make sure that money is worth it!

- This is how you should calculate your worth. If you want to earn $500,000 per year (Think BIG), calculate what you need to earn per day, per hour, and per minute. $500,000 a year = $1,369.86 per day, $57.08 per hour, and 95 cents a minute.

• When you walk into a new position with a solid sense of self-worth, you will know what kind of salary is acceptable and what is not. There is ZERO point working for a company that does not pay you what you are worth.

• Having said that–you will have to be realistic. If you are highly skilled and have a great track record, calculate accordingly. Do not overestimate your worth. It scales as you gain knowledge and will peak when you work for yourself one day.

• If you are doing a job that someone could be doing for $10 an hour, then that is what you think you are worth. Remedy it by searching for another job that pays you better.

Businesses will try and distract you from the fact that you are there to earn money. They will show you a great business culture, awesome people to work with, great free extras–anything to get you to want to work there for a little less.

Make no mistake, however; you are there to put cash dollars in your pocket. The only reason why I stuck with that horrible corn job was because it paid well. I guess you also have to balance what you are willing to do for money!

The High Worth Formula

You are your best asset, and to nurture and grow that asset, you must have a value and a future target that you would like to reach. This will help you plan for your future jobs, give you a timeline, and get you the money you eventually want to earn.

> *The high worth formula involves detailing your ideal target income so that you can work towards getting it. If you want to be earning a million dollars a year (THINK BIG), then that is the benchmark for your formula.*

- Document and record all of your successes (and failures) so that you have a current record of your worth as an employee. If a manager asks why you deserve a raise, you should be able to tell them exactly why you deserve one.

- Create an action blueprint to move up the ranks. If you are not working towards a promotion, then you are stagnant. There is no point in simply working for a paycheck. You need to work for more money.

- Find out what your title is and then outline the jobs you will need to secure in order to reach the top of your field. As you work, prove to your superiors that you are capable of leading, managing, and enforcing rules.

- Take your target earning amount and break it down into the separate categories that correlate with each title you need to achieve. If a million is impossible (short of becoming CEO), then at that stage you will leave and start your own company.

Do not forget to update your lifestyle according to your monetary goals. It is not likely that a senior manager will promote you to junior manager if you look like a teen fresh out of college. **Dress for the job you want, not the job you have.**

Setting Your Own Standards

Right now you have basic standards that govern what you will and will not accept in your job, boss, and company.

No one with self-esteem will accept a $1,000 pay cut with double the amount of work to do in a day. If you do, you are a patsy, and your company will ALWAYS take advantage of that. If you allow them to, they will work you to death and pay you nothing.

- Set your own standards. Having a salary figure in mind is a great way to ensure that you stay in the right earning bracket when looking for a new job.

- If you need things such as health insurance and dental to be covered by your company, make sure they are. These are important, life-changing decisions!

- Even when I took on the de-tasseling of corn job, I saw it as a learning experience. If the money is brilliant and there is an opportunity to learn something valuable, you can get away with doing it for a while.

- Remember you teach people how to treat you DURING work hours. Allowing a colleague to work with you and then claim the success as his own is not on. ***Never*** allow anyone to take advantage of you.

- If office politics backs you into a corner, always stand up for yourself. But do it in a non-violent, non-emotional, and extremely mature manner. No cursing and no petty talking behind other employees' backs. Always do the right thing to come off clean. Remember again, you never want to burn a bridge.

You are worth a lot more than you think. Companies cannot function without reliable, hard-working individuals. Individuals that know what they want are even more valuable, as they are the leaders of tomorrow. You have great value in your company–do not forget it!

09

Be Like a Pendulum

• • • • • • • •

"Nothing in this world can take the place of persistence. Talent will not; nothing is more common than unsuccessful men with talent. Genius will not; unrewarded genius is almost a proverb. Education will not; the world is full of educated derelicts. Persistence and determination alone are omnipotent."

Calvin Coolidge

One of the best pieces of advice I ever got was about persistence. "Be like a pendulum" that no matter what, will continue to swing back and forth, over and over again.

I am a firm believer in moving forward towards a goal, even if I have failed to achieve that goal many times before. Chances are I will achieve it one day. If I take failure to heart and stop, I will never achieve it. That is a fact.

When Mouths Like Melons: Job #8

My eighth job had me on the move, delivering fat, fresh watermelons off the back of a truck to hungry roadside customers.

They sold effortlessly and quickly; it was a dream sales scenario. When demand outweighs stock, you do not have to lift a finger to earn your money.

This job taught me to try and achieve an ideal sales scenario with anything that I sold so that sales would be effortless.

I tried to apply this principle to other products, but again and again I failed. What made the watermelon truck so popular? How could I replicate that?

- I narrowed it down to **timing, anticipation, and convenience.** Everyone knew where the watermelon truck was, how much they were, and when they came into season.

- People capitalized on the "freshness" of the watermelons by buying them from us. Our watermelons were quick to get on the way home from work or on the way to work in the morning.

You could buy a watermelon at any local grocery store in season, but people had the perception that we were selling watermelons right from the vine to their kitchen. Again, find a way to be unique from your competition.

Perception is a powerful thing in business. How you perceive people, for example, tells you how to respond to them. Perception creates your reality. You need to BE (dress, act) the person you want to be in order to succeed. People judge you within seven seconds of meeting you! As a female entrepreneur, this was a challenge, especially bashing through first impressions. The watermelon lesson never left me.

I am still trying to perfect my watermelon formula, but when it works–it really works. Effortless sales come from persistence, testing, retesting, and then doing it all over again.

Self-Awareness, Please

In order to become a more persistent person, allow me to let you in on a secret. You have to be acutely self-aware in order to become, and remain, a persistent person.

Persistence is not something you are born with; it is a skill that you learn. It combines motivation, vision, dreams, and drive into something you can see and feel in the real world.

- A self-aware person nurtures three main traits in order to become persistent: empathy, drive, and ego development. Another way of saying that is this: A self-aware person is able to better read others; has the drive to achieve and be the best; and will persevere through rejection, hardship, and struggle.

- Learn to identify and manage your innate strengths and weaknesses. If I was not a particularly nice person, being miserable while selling watermelons may have impacted business and caused some customers to not return.

- Examine your behaviors and try to become the ideal vessel for knowledge that can be used to meet your predefined goals. Being self-aware is a little bit like being self-obsessed, only you attempt to learn, change, and evolve for the good of your career.

- Learning self-awareness is like eating a watermelon. At first, it is tough to find the best way to open it up for inspection, but once you do, the rewards are great.

- Being self-aware is also a commitment to personal growth. Reading self-help books and learning about how to grow as an individual–mentally, spiritually, and physically–is all part of that.

A person that focuses on self-awareness as a career asset is someone that knows what he or she is doing. When you can improve yourself consistently, you have no limits. And this is only possible if you are able to gain insight about yourself and evolve over time.

Laughing in the Face of Danger

Persistence is not the easiest trait to learn and practice. You grow up believing that if you try hard enough, you will achieve success. But life does not always turn out that way.

Sometimes your best try is not good enough. Practicing persistence means laughing in the face of danger. There is always that risk that your hard work will not pay off.

I learned this my senior year in high school when I worked hard to be on the girls' varsity basketball team–I mean really hard–because I wanted it so much. Unfortunately, the coach cut me, and I was the only senior that was cut.

For no good reason, I was not allowed to be on that basketball team. This is the risk that persistence lays before you and why most people shy away from it.

- You cannot allow fear to prevent you from pursuing success like a bear that has followed a honey trail.

- Though being persistent does not always pay off, when it does, it is well worth it. When you have really worked hard for something and earned it, there is no better feeling than finally achieving that goal.

- Expect anything worth having to be extremely difficult to get. ***If you are not persistent, you will never achieve success.*** That is what you risk if you do not learn to practice persistence each and every day in your life.

- Laugh in the face of danger! Who cares if you take a risk and fail? Try again. It is only when you quit trying that you really fail.

If I could do it all over again, I would still try out for that basketball team. Because even though I did not make the team, I learned a valuable lesson from it.

> *Persistence does not always work out, but the alternative is far worse–instant failure.*

I'm Gonna Do It Anyway

Being persistent is about finding out what motivates you as a person. If you can remind yourself about the motivating factors that spur you to action, then you can start to take a more active role in your career.

Deciding to throw caution to the wind and be persistent anyway is the best decision you will ever make. But it comes at a cost.

- There are always unforeseen risks. No matter where you direct your persistent behavior, you have to accept the worst outcome is better than not trying your best to make it happen. Do it ANYWAY!

- Motivation is not a wispy, abstract concept. It is an action, which means that you have to **DO** it. Practicing motivation means ensuring that you meditate on your goals or find innovative ways to inspire yourself to be persistent.

- Identify what it is that you want and desire in life, love, work–everything. If you do not know where you are heading, you will not get there. I suggest making a long list of all the things you could ever possibly want. This is called a bucket list.

- Now make another list, a list called "what motivates me." Do not put your kids on there. I am talking about OTHER things that motivate you. If your best friend's new car motivates you to want to be able to afford one yourself–fine. Put it on the list!

- Have some discipline. When I say you should practice persistence and motivation, I mean you need to do it daily. Think of it as part of your success routine. Just having a success routine will make you more successful!

I have been practicing persistence for so long that I consider it part of my nature now. My other nickname is Persistent Pam! If you get to that point, you have done a great job! Remember, do not dwell on the risks. **As Nike says, just do it!**

The Road Less Travelled

Let us take a moment now to consider some hard truths. If success were easy, everyone would have it. Persistence is the key that unlocks success, so it makes sense that most people struggle to be persistent. They give up because that is easy.

I would encourage you to take the road less travelled. *There is no shortcut to success.* There is only working smart and working persistently towards your goals. Here is how to do that.

- *Believe that you can do it.* Who cares that no one in your family has ever earned a six-figure or even a seven-figure income! If your goal is to be super-rich, I believe that with enough persistence, you can make it happen.

- *Choose where to focus your persistence very carefully.* If you are going to make the effort, it might as well count. If you are after a promotion or starting a new business, set goals and apply your persistent nature there.

- *Do not forget to be passionate.* Passion drives motivation, which is the fuel of persistence. If you find yourself bored with what you are doing, it is not the goal that is boring you, it is the place. Move to another company. Learn from new people.

- *Choose fight over flight.* We all have a fight or flight response that kicks in when we do not feel good enough. Life loves to hold a mirror up to your face and poke fun at your dreams. Know your patterns. If you are prone to abandoning a sinking ship, then consciously decide not to.

- *Prove to yourself that you can do it.* Sometimes we need to prove things to ourselves before we can prove them to other people. Set a smaller goal, and use persistence to achieve it. Success will come quicker, and it will help motivate you to achieve your bigger goals.

Be persistent in every aspect of your life. It is the one single trait that **all** successful people have perfected. And it is one that you need to learn from today.

10

Eeek! Get It off Me!

● ● ● · · · ● ●

"I have learned over the years that when one's mind is made up, this diminishes fear; knowing what must be done does away with fear."

Rosa Parks

oubt and fear are real, and they prevents you from living the life that you deserve. FEAR is **F**alse **E**vidence **A**ppearing **R**eal. I like to imagine fear as a dangerous snake that rears up when you least expect it.

Learning to stamp on the snake's head every time this happens is a skill you need to learn. Do not allow the slithery, slimy scales of fear to hold you in their deathly grip. I hate snakes!

Scouts Honor, I Swear! Job #9

When you are young, sometimes you think you will like something that turns out to be a total nightmare. For me, the very embodiment of a nightmarish time was my ninth job–as a Girl Scout camp counselor.

It was a particularly hot and very humid Nebraska summer when I took on the position. Unfortunately, I was not a fan of camping. Or nights in total darkness. Or mice. Or spiders and snakes. Even the kids turned out to be too much to handle, and the responsibility started to terrify me.

- The entire time I worked as a counselor, I was out of my comfort zone, and it forced me to face my fears. At that time, it seemed as though all of my worst fears were around me. My only option was to move past them.

- I learned that fear spirals out of control when you feed it. When you stop and logically look at your fear, there is very little that actually threatens you.

- I was in a leadership position and had to be strong for the kids. This helped me see past the irrational thoughts that tend to buzz in your mind, like a hive of bees that are determined to make you panic.

Shifting Perspectives: The 3D View

Fear is a funny thing. One of the first things I was ever afraid of was water. We used to travel by car nearly 1,300 miles and two days on the highways from Nebraska to Florida every year as a family to visit my grandfather's three sisters and cousins in Jacksonville. The car was always muggy because we did not have any air conditioning.

The road trip made for great childhood memories–driving the long way from Omaha to Jacksonville in an old station wagon. We loved it. Leaving the flat state to head down to the sunny beach every year was a treat.

One year when we had been cruising around Daytona Beach–playing and swimming–a huge wave knocked me over, and I was sucked under the water for what seemed like a vivid, misted blue eternity.

When I eventually surfaced and we left the beach, I knew something had changed. A single terrified moment and I had developed a fear of water. Life will get you like that.

That is why you need to learn to shift your perspectives about fear and adopt a 3D view of it.

- *Fear is often illogical and unreasonable.* If you are going to overcome it, you need to learn to step back from your fear to see if it really threatens you. Most of the time, fear is intangible, such as the fear of failure.

- *Turn fear into action.* If fear overwhelms you, sit down and make a list of steps that you can take to alleviate this fear. Even a simple escape strategy can make you feel more secure. Nothing is worse than the fear itself!

- *Learn to be more courageous.* When you notice yourself being fearful for no reason, treat it as a call to action. Afraid of failing? Work hard not to fail. Afraid of your boss? Address the reasons why, and deal with them. Do not run away from your fear.

Network Marketing or Bust

Network marketing was always something I really enjoyed doing. Meeting new people and getting to know them was fun for me. But I quickly recognized many other people did not feel that way.

There must be hundreds of people-related fears in existence. You are scared of letting people down, being seen as a failure, messing up, not being liked–I mean, the list goes on and on. But a fear of network marketing is one fear you cannot afford to have.

- Network marketing and direct sales involve meeting and dealing with a lot of people. More than that, they concern selling things to those people. That is enough to terrify anyone, and it is a common fear.

- Public speaking has always ranked among the most common fears in the world. But I like to call these fears "faux fears" because they are not real. People are actually really nice, and they want to hear what you have to say!

- The more people you know, the better off you will be in your career. People help make other people successful. It is as simple as that. Being afraid to deal with people or avoiding it is not a constructive way to move forward in business. As the saying goes, "It is not what you know, but who you know," or "Not who you know, but who knows you" works most of the time.

- Networking is not as scary as you think. Even if you begin with meeting just one person at an event, it can help your career. If I want to start a conversation with someone I just met, the question that always works is "Where did you grow up?" Not "Where are you from?" People love to talk about where they grew up and go back in time to talk about a favorite memory.

- If you do not learn to be good with people, you will sacrifice a huge part of your potential to be successful. If you think it is hard gaining success, wait until you try to achieve it all on your own!

> *Your marketing power grows with your network, which means the more people you know, the more money you will make as a business owner. Do not allow your people "faux fear" to get in the way of real success.*

The Network of Authority

There is real authority in networking. These days the Internet can help you gain authority, but back then, all you had was networking events.

- Wear your nametag on the right side of your jacket so that when you shake someone's hand, they can read your name as you introduce yourself.

- Crowds always made me a bit nervous. I tried to negate those fears by scanning the crowd, finding someone I had met before, and making a beeline towards them. Now, today, I enjoy meeting new people at events.

- Get to know your network contacts. They should not be acquaintances. They should be friends. Begin by asking questions that illicit a yes or no response to make it easy for them. Follow with questions about their childhood, where they are from, and what their upbringing was like.

- Most people at networking events are only there to talk business. They do not care WHO you are. You can differentiate yourself by caring about the people you meet. They will convert into contacts far quicker than focusing purely on business. People want to do business with people, not brands.

- Leadership is about being confident and making the first move. It does not matter if you are nervous or fumbly. People understand that. But if you hide in the shadows because you are shy, you will never be seen as a leader.

Finding Uncommon Commonalities

Uncommon commonalities are something a very good friend taught me about when we would attend events together. It is a way to connect with complete strangers by finding "uncommon" common ground.

As people, we connect with each other based on the experiences we have shared, the things we like or dislike, and the way we are. At networking events or in team building scenarios, it can be difficult finding common ground with people unless you use these techniques.

- The goal of a meeting would be to create a list of different things that everyone likes and dislikes according to a certain context. For example, "things you like to do on a Saturday."

- The next step would be to pair off and see who you have the most in common with. Even one small thing that you have in common can spark a great working relationship. You can always come back to it in conversation.

- At a networking event, you can casually mention an experience you have had and see if anyone else shares your experience. Using this method of connection, you will attract like-minded people to you, and then you can convert them into network contacts.

- Recognizing and appreciating what other people like to do is a great ice-breaker in any networking scenario. Do not stick exclusively to that topic, but use it as a stepping stone for moving forward with the relationship and meeting other people through your new contact.

- Always, always, always FOLLOW UP with the person you would like to establish a personal or business relationship with by making a phone call or sending an email to set up a coffee or lunch meeting. ***Remember –fortune is in the follow-up!***

Challenge What You Think You Know

Fear is often based on bad experiences that are unlikely to occur again. Did you see the episode of *The Oprah Show* where Tony Robbins' *Unleash the Power Within* made her walk over hot coals? The Firewalk is intended as the ultimate metaphor to let you experience that what holds you back and what you are afraid of is often easier to overcome than you think.

It is all about learning to control your mind and the thoughts that go on in there. To control fear, you need to control your mind. My husband and I went on a trip to the country of Belize in Central America recently with a very fun couple in our neighborhood–Kevin and Maria Telfer–for our 15-year wedding anniversaries, and thought I would have to face dozens of my most guarded fears.

- After a direct flight from Dallas to Belize City, we had to board a tiny, 20-person plane to reach the resort. Any sane person will see a small plane and recall those Hollywood movies where everyone always dies. I was afraid.

- I made a conscious decision to leave my fears behind in Dallas. I let go of it, and it slithered away. You have to realize that being afraid is not going to help you survive a plane crash; it only makes the ride completely horrible.

- Because I managed to release my fear, I could enjoy the incredible Caribbean Sea for the first time. I had a really good flight and decided from then on that I would not let any fear paralyze me on that vacation.

- My fears were many: the tall, black man with a marijuana leaf symbol on his hat who picked us up at our meeting point standing next to his very well-traveled, dusty, old blue van to take us on an excursion of the Belize countryside; cave tubing; the jungle; deadly mosquito bites; cave claustrophobia; darkness; and water. They were all around me, but I let them go to experience the adventure of it all. I kept telling myself that I would need to stop my mind from crazy thoughts and to enjoy the moment. I was thrilled to conquer my fears head on and felt the freedom rushing throughout me. I was a new person.

To this day, Maria and I laugh about the fears and adventures we had together on that fabulous trip to Belize. When you share your fears and say them out loud to a friend, it is amazing how the fear has no more power. If you live in fear, you will NEVER experience all of the opportunities to enjoy life.

This is really how we are in everyday life–full of fear. All you have to do is read the daily news events or turn on the news to create additional fear. It molds our actions and holds us back. But I did not die of a tropical disease; I did not drown or get hauled away by bats; and our guide was a very entertaining native. I was fine, and I had one of the best memories of a lifetime. The lesson?

Challenge what you think you know about your fears. Most of the time, they are just thoughts. And thoughts can be forgotten.

The Risk vs. Rewards Problem

In every fearful situation in life, there is a risk vs. rewards scenario. If you are afraid of something, it is usually because it can harm you in some way. On the other hand, letting go of that fear can result in a surplus of surprising rewards.

You have to learn to weigh up your pressing fears with the rewards they are actively hiding away from you. ***Do not let fear control where your future is heading.***

- Many people are afraid of failure, but on closer inspection, they are actually afraid of success. For whatever reason, they have convinced themselves they are not good enough and use "failure" as an excuse not to press forward.

- Worst case scenarios almost never happen. Seriously! When was the last time something really horrid happened to you? Fear is mostly a mental stressor, not a physical threat. Step back and say, what are the chances? Then move on.

- Best case scenarios are way more common than worst case scenarios. Just like you can work towards the best case, you can ensure the worst case does not happen to reduce your worry by taking action to release your fear.

- All fear comes with a certain amount of risk. When you are truly afraid of something, you think it is going to get you 24/7. Let us be honest–that is silly! A spider is not going to plan to attack you. Darkness comes each night. And that promotion you are terrified to ask for is going to someone; it might as well be you.

To overcome fear, all you need in life is a spot of courage and some clarity. Take a deep breath. Calm yourself. If you know you are being ridiculous, consciously release the fear. It is not going to help you. In fact, it is better to face fear head on, so the more fears you have, the more you will have to face.

11

Laws about Time Travel

● ● · · · ● ●

"Time is the coin of your life. It is the only coin you have, and only you can determine how it will be spent. Be careful lest you let other people spend it for you."
Carl Sandburg

How much do you value your time? Most people do not even want to think about how old they are and what time they have left.

But time is ticking away whether you use it efficiently or not. And most successful business people are time management professionals. They know what their time is worth.

Food So Fast It Runs: Job #10

Job number 10 was an eye opener. I had eaten at a lot of fast food places before, but I never quite understood how difficult it was to be the person behind the counter.

I took the job at Arby's when I was 16 for minimum wage at a pay rate of $3.35 per hour to learn about the fast food industry. In no time at all I was in a fast food whirlwind of training, customer service, cooking, procedures, cleaning up, and non-stop shifts. It was something of a rude awakening for a 16-year-old. I highly recommend every young person should work at a fast food job to learn how difficult the low paying job really is, but the experience was very valuable.

- Before I worked at Arby's, I believed that fast food was a term for the food, but once I had done my first long shift, I had a new definition. Everything in that place was done quickly, efficiently, and according to certain posted rules. Time was of the essence.

- I started thinking about how hard I had to work for so little money. The customer was the one getting the real benefit here. I was learning a great deal about customer service, cooking the roast beef right, and cleaning–our boss always told us, "If you have time to lean, you have time to clean." That has always stuck with me.

- Working in a fast food restaurant teaches you how to work at a fast pace on your feet for long shifts, and the customer is ALWAYS right!

One Cent for a Minute

When I worked over at Arby's, I realized pretty quickly that even though the pay was low–and the job was hard–it was also high stress. Things had to move along at a certain speed in order for people to leave as satisfied customers.

I learned something fundamental that has helped me develop my time management ability over the years–time is not free. There is a direct sale that goes on that employers do not like to talk about. Time is priceless, sure, but they will offer you a buck an hour for it.

- There is some truth to the saying "If you do not value yourself, you cannot value your time." We are all born with a certain amount of time on the clock. You can choose to ignore it or optimize it.

- Time has real value–the kind that no amount of money can afford to buy. But we are forced to sell it for income. That is why you need to think really hard about how much your time is worth. Being underpaid is poor planning, that is all.

- When you set goals and reach for more in your life and career, you focus your energy on optimizing your time. Being aimless and moving through life with no plan does not result in happiness. In fact, people that do not plan lack fulfillment and purpose.

- The whole concept behind "intentional" living is to gain perspective about your life. Time is an important element, and it affects you in so many ways. You should never, ever give your time away for nothing.

It is funny how we will drive a half an hour out of our way to complain about a burger without cheese on it from our local fast food restaurant–but we struggle to demand what our time is worth from our employer.

The Money Tree

Trading time for money directly is not a great formula for success if you are working in a 9–5. No one has enough experience at the beginning of their careers to make this conversion worth it. But we all have to do it; it is the most popular way to earn money, after all.

Remember when your father used to say, "Money does not grow on trees"? This kind of negative attitude towards success and money is what got you in your 9–5 in the first place, working all of your time away for next to nothing. That has to change.

- Look at where you work. If the commute is taking you too long, then you are losing valuable time and money. Moving closer to your job can boost your income, so you may want to consider it.

- Look at what you do. When you do eventually own your own company, do not be afraid to charge for transport costs and time spent traveling. Just five hours a week in a car adds up to 50 weeks in a year with over 250 hours that you should bill for. Short changing yourself is not a good life strategy.

- Other people value your time as you value your time. If you give your boss lots of free hours of overtime, expect lots more of it in your near future. Companies will always take advantage of a willing asset.

- You need to learn about time strategy and management. People that do not observe that their time is valuable fail to plan their weeks. As a result, you will begin to habitually be overworked and underpaid, and you will habitually miss out on opportunities to improve in your career.

Money may not grow on trees, but there is a lot of it in the world. There is no imagined "scarcity" like the saying suggests. If you learn to value your time better and manage it more efficiently, you can enjoy much higher work satisfaction in your daily life.

From the Finite Perspective

You can always tell who values their time and who does not in a work environment. You cannot physically sacrifice your health or career for meager earnings, yet this is exactly what most people do. That is why you have to see time from a finite perspective.

- Your time to succeed is limited. You do not have an endless amount of time stretched out before you that can be accessed at any point. Time is not infinite; it is finite.

- Calculate how you spend your time. It takes the first 20 years of your life to grow up, and by the age of 60, you want to be able to retire fairly soon. That leaves you with 40 years–minus "finding yourself time," and realistically, it is more like 20 years.

- You need to learn to manage the expectations of the people around you. In your job, they need to know what you are prepared to do for money and what you will not sacrifice your time for. This will give your managers more respect for you!

- Everything has a purpose. You will find that people that effectively manage their time use all the tools and advice at their disposal. They are always on time, and they set goals to every aspect of their daily living. As a result, they speed ahead and learn to portion their time carefully for every pre-defined purpose.

Time by its very nature is relentless, and yet there is a definite end we must all meet one day. Will you look back and think, I could have done more with my time? Start by thinking, "My time is worth more," and you will adjust your earnings accordingly.

And Tonight...a Time Machine

Though you live your life like you have a time machine in your yard for emergencies, this is not the case in the real world. Once a day has passed, it is gone. Every second you are getting older and hopefully wiser–but it begins with a healthy respect for the march of time.

If a time machine could take you back, which parts of your life would you do over?

> *It is never too late to recognize that time is your most important commodity.*

- In a recent survey of 3,200 people, 64% say that they visit websites unrelated to work on a daily basis. People will naturally try to fill their time with entertainment unless their time is being valued properly.

- If you waste time at work, you do not value your time. Then you are just trying to get through the day so that you can collect your pay check. There is NOTHING worse than purposefully wishing your time away.

- Work is called work because it is not always fun to do. Until you are trained up and working for yourself, you have to apportion your time very carefully so that you can grow as a business person. Do not allow your bosses to take advantage of this.

- Real freedom is when you do not have to trade time for money. This happens when you are earning passive income or major income in a job where you are able to delegate your time. Many wealthy people all over the world can stop working, yet money will flow into their accounts. Money works for them. Money never sleeps!

I will never forget first watching that film *Back to the Future* with Michael J. Fox. I remember thinking, "Wow, I wish time machines were real." But the truth is that life is not about "do-overs." You get one shot at success with the time you are given. Learn the lesson now and save yourself a lot of wasted time.

12

The Love Hate Relationship

● ● ● · · · ● ●

"I believe you are your work.
Don't trade the stuff of your
life, time, for nothing more than
dollars. That's a rotten bargain."
Rita Mae Brown

It took me years to find my niche–the one I knew that I would love forever. Everything before that was training for the main event–owning my own business.

Work has always inspired love/hate relationships in people. I believe if you cannot find a job that you LOVE to do, you have not looked hard enough for it.

Tools for a Better Future: Job #11

My eleventh job was something special. I needed the money, so I took a cashier job at Handy Andy Home Improvement Center, the big box hardware store. I loved it there from the very beginning.

It was great helping friendly clients find what they needed. I was trusted with the task and took my responsibility seriously. I learned to be the friendly cashier checking out every type of imaginable type of lumber, tools, hardware, garden supplies– you name it, this place carried it for their customers. The people there made the work fun.

- I learned that even small, monotonous jobs can be incredible with the right company, philosophy, and setting. I was not a whizz with tools or anything, and most of the time I did not know what I was ringing up, but I learned, and it was really enjoyable at the time.

• My job at Handy Andy's taught me there is a tool for everything. And if the tool did not exist, one could be fashioned from other tools. It was a metaphor for fixing the problems in my life, specifically in my career.

• We all need a reason to get out of bed in the morning. If that reason is your job–because you love it so much– success will naturally follow. Most people hate what they do, and work becomes a kind of social torture.

Think about the last work-related thing you really enjoyed. Would it not be amazing if every day was dedicated to doing something you loved?

The Hidden Purpose Handbook

Life is not strictly about your career; it involves other factors: relationships, family, home, and travel. It seems to be the first question someone asks you when they first meet you. What do you do, or where do you work? But it is your career that helps you gain that sense of purpose in life. I believe that if you find a job that you love, it must be connected with your life purpose.

• *To find your purpose, take action.* **You have to act to get results.** Do not make excuses for yourself anymore. It may be easier to take the elevator than the stairs, but the stairs will teach you more about the heights that you can reach.

- *Focus on your core skills.* If you are going to find a job that you love to do, it should be involved with your core skills–the ones you like to use every day. If you like to work on the computer a lot, for example, find a job that allows you to do this.

- *Your hidden purpose is already happening.* Whether you know it or not, **everyone has a purpose**. You can ignore your purpose and waste your time, but your life will still move forward. That is nature. Why not actively seek out your purpose so that you have some control over it instead?

- *Gaining experience is part of your journey.* No matter where you work or what you do, there is always a lesson to take away from an experience. To become wise, you must seek out these lessons and use them to evolve as a person.

- *Purpose is not a singular term.* Stop thinking of your purpose as a single item destination that you will reach one day. Your purpose is multi-faceted and dynamic. It changes as you change. So make sure you are always learning so you can find the things you love in any position.

Say No to Boredom

I quickly discovered a pervasive lean towards being bored in many of the jobs that I took on. After I had learned all I could, the monotony of the daily drill would hang me out to dry like a tatty washcloth. I hated it!

There is no reason to be bored at work. Boredom is the great instigator of time wasting when you could be doing something for the good of your career. Instead, remember your goal here is to learn to love what you do…eventually.

- *Your surroundings affect your mood.* Wherever you are, create a small space just for you. In a corporate job, that would mean decorating your office or cubicle a little with your own personality. You will not be as bored if your office area feels more like home. I like the beach, palm trees, and bright colors, so I fill my space with those types of items.

- *Do not allow boredom to distract you.* Often boredom begins when you are working. You will take a break and then become distracted–losing yourself on the Internet or doing something other than what you should be doing. Be aware of this. **Again, remember time is money!**

- *Say no to boredom.* Boredom does not help you get ahead. It fills your mind with fluff and makes you lazy. When you feel bored, work on your schedule or focus on one of the other skills that will help you find your eventual dream job.

- *Use the FOCUS process.* **F**ollow **O**ne **C**ourse **U**ntil **S**uccessful, then follow up on it. If your goal for the day is to make money, then zone in on it. Make it a top priority, and work towards that singular goal. Sometimes laser focus can eliminate boredom because it simplifies what you have to do–making it more enjoyable.

> *Boredom is not a skill; it is a side effect of not having a solid plan or purpose.*

If you are going to find happiness in your job or in a job that you have in the future, you have got to learn to take responsibility for what you do while "working."

No One Kicks a Dead Dog

When I was working at Handy Andy's, although I absolutely loved my job, I worked with some people who did not feel the same way. There was one man in particular who did not take kindly to being asked to do ANYTHING, even if it was perfectly within his job description.

This guy was constantly bored. He barely worked, and he was always involved in some kind of drama with his girlfriend. No one ever asked him for help. They assumed he was happy being a slacker with no purpose, and they let him be. No one kicks a dead dog.

- *You project what you feel.* If you hate your job, it shows. People will not want to engage with you as much, which limits your growth opportunities. When you love your job, that passion is felt by all. People flock to you, and they engage. Have you ever been to the World Famous "Pike Place Fish Market" in Seattle, WA, where fishmongers throw fish and have fun with the customers? Now, they know how to have **FUN** at work!

- *Find challenges and overcome them.* If you do not want to be seen as a "dead dog" of your office or workplace, actively look for challenges. Spot problems, and come up with solutions. **Get noticed**. Do not be afraid to be brilliant.

- *The workplace should be a fun zone.* Sometimes there are good reasons why businesses do not allow you to let your hair down at work. But most of the time when you add an element of fun to a project, it speeds things along. Working at Handy Andy's was so much fun that it did not feel like work at all.

- *Keep a performance chart.* If you are serious about optimizing yourself for your future, then perhaps you should keep a performance chart. At the end of your work day, evaluate how you did. Record your emotions, what happened on the day, what you learned, and how you can improve.

If people are avoiding you at work, it may be because they can see that you hate your job. Hate pushes people away; love pulls them closer. You do not want to be labeled the dead dog in the office. These people are terrible to be around because of their lackluster attitude.

A Cold Serving of Criticism

Because of the 25 jobs I have held down, I know all about working with different bosses–and the criticism that can come your way. Attitude is a very important part of work, although it is not spoken about as often as it should be.

When you show up at work bored and lazy, expect more criticism from those around you. Negative mindsets at work attract criticism and problems. Being positive and searching for solutions does the opposite; it attracts help, support, and complements.

- *Keep your job in perspective.* If it is a stepping stone, then do not act as if you are going to be stuck in it for 20 years. Perk up, be positive, and learn to find the good in the positions you get.

- *Learn to deal with criticism.* All jobs come with different levels of criticism according to your experience level, boss, and co-workers. If you love your job, you can keep this criticism to a minimum and get on with your day.

- *Listen to all criticisms.* Sometimes a boss or co-worker will try to get through to you by criticizing something that you have done. Listen to what they are saying to see if they are right. Record your lesson and how you can prevent a similar criticism in future.

- *Some criticism has nothing to do with you.* I had a boss once who liked to serve up a cold plate of criticism daily to everyone that worked for him. I figured out he just had a control complex, and there was nothing of value in his ramblings. Not all criticisms are worth listening to.

> *Your job is to prime yourself for your ideal job that you will love. To do this, you have to work with a few frogs before you are hired by your dream boss.*

13

A Skydiver's Guide to Failure

•••••••

"When you get into a tight place and everything goes against you, still it seems as though you could not hang on a minute longer, never give up then, for that is just the place and time that the tide will turn."

Harriet Beecher Stowe

S kydivers know a thing or two about failure. They make sure it does not happen! When a skydiver fails, they die. For us, things may be equally as dire, only we cannot see it yet.

If you are in the habit of giving up, you are not alone.

> *What makes a person successful is the drive to never give up, to never let the world pull you down and under.*

From Russia with Love, Cat: Jobs #12&13

My next two jobs (#12 and #13) during college breaks were epic and interesting, far better than my fast food gig. First, I got a job at the largest home furnishings store in North America called Nebraska Furniture Mart. It was not your average job; I learned how to arrange the accessories around the showroom with the famous owner, Mrs. B (Rose Blumkin).

Mrs. B was an immigrant from Russia who moved to the United States to find her American dream. On a $500 investment, Mrs. B started the furniture, flooring, appliances, and electronics store, and under the motto "sell cheap and tell the truth," she worked in the business until age 103. It was really inspiring to hear her story, and it resonated with the stories that my grandmother used to tell us about her immigration.

The job I held after that was at Catfish Lake, working in my father's restaurant. Everyone seems to have the dream of owning their own restaurant. Trust me, it is not all as glamorous as seen on television shows. At both places, there were challenges to overcome. This is what I learned.

- Even when you live in Russia with nothing, there are ways to achieve your dream. All you need are guts and a plan.

- Customers can be nice, and they can be mean. People bring their emotions with them when they go shopping. Staff are people too.

- All I could do was my best for just a summer job. As a result, I learned a lot about customer service and running a business successfully.

- All jobs can be temporary, so enjoy the short time of meeting new people and learning from the experience.

Success Is Failure Inside Out

School trains you to fear failure, and this fear can continue through your life–ironically causing the failure you have been so afraid of falling prey to. But success is always on the horizon if you get into the habit of setting goals and achieving them.

I like to think of success as failure turned inside out. Instead of being scared to fail, I look at it as a healthy appreciation; if I do not succeed, my life will be very difficult. As a result, I try not to fail at succeeding!

- I used to watch a lot of *The Oprah Show*, and she would always say that failure is just an invented concept; it is not real. Because what is failure anyway but a resistance to keep reaching for success?

- Success offers clarity, while failure offers uncertainty. If you give up, you will never find your way to the right answer. Focusing on success instead of failure can help you unearth the answers that you have been searching for.

- Success provides inspiration, while failure brings desperation. If you focus on success instead, you will always be able to move forward. Focus on failure, and you will end up compromising on your goals just to survive.

- Success aids commitment, while failure gives you permission to do nothing. Honing in on success instead of failure will help you inch towards your goals. If you give up and quit, there is zero chance of you ever reaching your goals.

Take it from a Michael Jordan quote on Success Through Failure, "*I've missed 9000 shots in my career. I've lost almost 300 games. 26 times, I've been trusted to take the game winning shot and missed. I've failed over and over and over again in my life. And that is why I succeed."*

> **Remove failure from your vocabulary; it has no positive place in your life.**

Instead, become someone who is dedicated to success, even though it will take a while to achieve. With no chance of failure, you will be able to experience the real power of never giving up.

The Loser Mentality

A loser is someone who has been identified as having potential but has made the decision to waste this potential consistently throughout his or her life. I have discovered that many people have variations of this complex, which gives them permission to quit.

If a skydiver decided it was too much trouble one day to check all of the parachutes, to train, and to make sure the aircraft is 100% ready for the trip, bad things would happen. Why do our lives mean any less than this? We are all packing parachutes every day on the road to success. Those that do not will end up a smudge on the sidewalk.

- My personal motto has always been to follow Winston Churchill's famous quote of **Never, Never, Never Give Up**. You never know when a major breakthrough is going to happen that will change your life. All you can do until then is soldier on.

- Losers love to complain about their lives, but they never take **ACTION** to change it for the better. Only you have the power to affect your future. If you want it to be great, then your present needs a revamp.

- Save the drama, mama. I have noticed that people with a loser mentality are entitled people who love to attract drama and make it everyone's business. Insecurity can only be masked with drama for so long. Decide to never give up, and you will have no excuses for your behavior.

- Being self-absorbed, pessimistic, and lazy are all traits that someone with a loser mentality has fostered. You can turn this mentality around with that one simple decision! Take up your pursuit of success again, and you will not be a failure or a loser.

The loser mentality is widespread in workplaces all over the country. But just because other people are comfortable with their bad attitudes does not mean you should be. Not giving up is a full-time job. Life will continue to try and get the better of you, but you have to fight back with every tool you have!

Help! Help! This Is My Life

I struggle to imagine what it must have been like for Mrs. B, moving from Russia to the U.S. to find a better life. But I have woken up one day in panic. I have thought, "Oh my gosh, this is my life." And life is what you make it.

The catch, of course, is that for the first few decades, you have no idea how to make it, and finding out is a huge learning curve. Those that do discover how to succeed are able to look back on their journey with pride. Those that do not—well, that should not happen to you.

- Take stock of your life as it is right now. Do you have regrets? It is **never** too late to decide that you want to be successful. All you have to do is start trying again—I mean really trying—with purpose.

- All success takes time. It is impossible to gain success overnight, even in an "overnight success" scenario. People that make it that way take several months or years to perfect their overnight success formula.

- To improve your job, focus on your customers. Giving them great service is training for the future. Even today I make sure all of my clients are happy.

We once stayed at the luxury Ritz-Carlton resort in Truckee, CA, (Lake Tahoe) one summer, and that evening someone knocked at the door holding a large silver platter with a white gift-wrapped package. We were not expecting a gift from anyone. The boys ripped the package opened so quickly to find a package of marshmallows, graham crackers, and a lot of chocolate bars. The gift was from the hotel manager, who was welcoming us for staying there a second time and wanted us to enjoy smores by their fire pits. We were so impressed they remembered that we stayed with them before, and to provide a nice gift unexpectedly was a HUGE surprise. It does not take much, but people want to be remembered.

- Stop comparing your life to other people. They are not you, and they have not had to face the same challenges you have had to face. For you, success may take six years–or it may take three months. Pursue it earnestly and find out.

General Lack

In a military situation, there are only two outcomes: success or failure. Achieving success is difficult because it requires exact timing, hard work, and collaboration. If all of the methods for success fail and time runs out, that is when the mission is declared a failure.

Your life is your mission. You have a timeline with an uncertain end. Who would you rather have in charge of your forces–General Abundance or General Lack? They lead to two very different roads. Oh, and if you do not choose, you automatically get General Lack.

- *Dealing with General Lack.* When you feel like a failure, it is hard to stay motivated to do anything positive. A general lack of interest takes hold, and the rest of your life plummets into stagnancy or wasteful oblivion.

- *Being promoted to General Abundance.* When you make the decision to never give up, you attract general abundance into your life. Positivity, challenges, and success are all linked to abundance and will follow.

- *At Nebraska Furniture Mart, they took a negative and turned it into a positive.* This is the very definition of not giving up. I remember a very clever advertisement that Nebraska Furniture Mart took out in the newspaper to get HUGE attention; they created a "going out FOR business sale." Everyone thought it was a "going out OF business" sale with such low prices, but it was not. It was very successful.

- *Do not allow General Lack to take over your life.* Lower your expectations, become stronger, persist, and **fake it until you make it**! As long as General Abundance is leading your thoughts, there is nothing to worry about. You will succeed as long as you are driving towards that goal.

Giving up is something we do so easily these days. We give up on business, on careers, on dreams, and on marriage. We struggle to stick to one path, and we blame ourselves for it. Make the decision to **NEVER** give up, and you will not have to deal with the negative consequences of allowing General Lack to run your life. He always loses.

14

Ain't No Mountain Higher

● ● ● · · ● ●

"Don't think. Thinking is the enemy
of creativity. It's self-conscious, and
anything self-conscious is lousy.
You can't try to do things. You
simply must do things."

Ray Bradbury

Creativity is something that everyone has but few people practice. Thirty years ago only artists and designers were thought to be creative. Now everyone in business needs creativity.

There is no mountain higher than the lofty goals involved with creativity. But being creative is an essential stepping stone to success—a trait that you must foster from early on.

Pizza and Spring Break: Job #14

My 14th job was really split into three parts during college: the work I did at the student union, a pizza place position, and selling trips down to Daytona Beach, Florida for spring break.

- When I worked at the student union in college, I loved reading the free magazines. People would stop by and chat; it was fun. There was a real sense of community and creativity in the air.

- Valentino's Pizza supported me while I was in college. I had to make sure that the salad bar never ran out of salad. To do this, I had to walk from the hot kitchen into a freezing cooler—it was not my favorite. The pizza was incredible and is still my favorite to this day. The work was hard, but I learned that people expected the food to be consistent at every visit. It was a fun part-time job.

- I decided to respond to an ad in the college paper looking for people to organize trips to Daytona Beach, FL, during spring break for college students. I knew Daytona Beach well, so I really sold them on the place. I thought a few people would come, but I ended up with three bus loads.

- It was hard work, but I managed to find creative solutions for minor problems. For example, I gave four free trips to the people that helped me organize it all. In the end, I earned about $2,000 from it. That seemed like a ton of money back in 1985 for just a short time of planning.

Look Behind, but Think Ahead

A creative person is always trying to find new and innovative ways to solve problems. This has become a major skill in the corporate world, so it is an asset you need to work on every day.

Think of creativity as a portal. It is made up of all the things you have learned in your past, which are then processed and turned into insights for your future. You will constantly move forward along the timeline, gaining experience and enhancing your creative attributes.

- *Look into your past for clues.* How have you been creative in your past? How can you express this creativity in your current job? A creative individual is great at setting goals and then reaching them via innovative means.

- *Look to your future for skill development.* Based on the jobs you have had and the skills that you have accrued, what do you still need to learn to be the best at what you love? That is the million dollar question.

- *Opportunities only arise for creative types that are actively looking for them.* A misfiled folder that keeps becoming lost is an opportunity for someone with initiative to come up with a better system to solve that recurring problem.

- *Get faster response times.* You will often find that creative individuals respond to challenges faster, as they are eager to get to the brainstorming and testing process. When you can think laterally about a problem, the problem will not last for long.

To improve your creativity portal, all you need is time and good decision making ability. Every place you work and every person you meet will influence you in some small way. The key is to choose the right learning areas so that you can develop quickly into a powerfully creative person who always has the answers.

I have always considered myself to be a very creative person. If everyone is doing something one way, I will find a way to make my idea or project stand out. One time for a group presentation, I decided I needed to stand out in the group and remembered that for my boys' birthday parties, I would order a sheet cake with their pictures on the top. I did the same thing with my marketing brochure and presented it to the group to eat. You must be UNIQUE!

Working with the Mystery Box

I am sure that you have heard about the mystery box–the one we are always told to think outside of: "Think outside the box." Thinking outside the box is a uniquely creative endeavor that happens when a business or individual needs a fresh solution to an old problem. Two of the most creative people (in my opinion) were and are Steve Jobs with Apple Computer and Richard Branson with Virgin Airlines. Both of these men have changed the world.

The trouble is most people do not even realize what the "box" is or how they think while inside it. The term commonly refers to the ability to use unconventional thinking to solve problems as opposed to traditional thinking, which renders unusable results.

- *Run through your creative process.* First identify the issue, then list the solutions that are typical when working with that issue. Next, map out how to improve the issue and brainstorm what could work. Be as lateral as you like.

- *Learn through multiple industries.* If there is one thing I have learned, it is to think outside of the box. When you work in many industries, you get exposed to different processes, modes of thought, and business methods. The more you know, the easier it is to apply lateral thought to a problem.

- *Do something unusual in a business context.* If you are stuck in a boardroom and do not feel inspired, take turns doing something unusual and getting inspired. Often if you are the person doing the inspiring, it gets others to contribute to outside the box thinking, and you can crowd source a solution.

In my life, there have been many opportunities when the ability to think creatively has come in handy. I do believe it is a trait everyone should work on, and evolve with, in their lives. There is nothing worse than a person that does not have an original thought, never contributes, and could not care less about problem-solving.

Creative Assassins

In the workplace, you will discover that there are creative assassins everywhere. They hide like ninjas in your pot plants and pencil holders, waiting to empty your brain of any creative ideas for the day. Be aware of these, and take steps to eliminate them.

A creative assassin is something in your immediate vicinity that will kill your creative thought processes. Any number of things can induce this state so beware.

- According to Harvard University, one of the biggest creativity assassins is a role mismatch. If people are placed in roles they are not suited for, it will crush their creative thought processes and result in stress and even panic.

- Limited resources and time kill creativity. If the company you work for overloads you with work and then gives you 30 minutes of meeting time–while expecting a creative solution–they are probably deluded.

- A total lack of social diversity hurts creativity. The best way to get a number of different opinions is to include them in the creative process. This is why so many businesses push diversity–because people from different backgrounds notice different things.

- An absence of positive feedback and reinforcement stifles people. If no one even mentions what a great job you did on the last project, your next one will not be as good. People need acceptance and positive feedback from their bosses. If they do not get it, they will not feel motivated to do their best again.

There are other factors, such as goal-restriction and a lack of support, that will sneak in and assassinate any creativity in your head. You should be aware that people, location, mood, drive, and feedback all affect how creative someone can be.

EQ and IQ: What?

Forbes recently spoke about IQ and how in the old days it was important to have a high IQ to reach the top tiers of your career. These days a new form of intelligence has cropped up that supports creativity and the advancement of your career.

- EQ, or emotional IQ, is crucial to your creativity levels. Some 85% of your financial success is due to skills associated with EQ, including your leadership skill, negotiation ability, communication skills, and personality.

- MQ, or moral intelligence, also affects creativity. Your specific code of ethics and built-in moral center helps you make decisions concerning your career. Based on this, you will need to develop your integrity, sympathy, capacity for forgiveness, and responsibility in order to enhance your creative side.

- BQ, or body intelligence, involves how you feel about your body, how you take care of it, and how well you know it. This affects your thoughts, self-confidence, energy levels, and state of mind–all important factors when being creative.

- Real success is a combination of developing your EQ, MQ, and BQ. It just does not matter if you have an IQ of 100 or 160. You do not need to be highly educated in order to succeed. All you need is training, experience, and a willingness to push the boundaries of what we consider to be "creative" solutions at work.

• Be aware of your inner voice. This governs your EQ, and it can be controlled and trained. If you are not inspired, for example, you can always find ways to become inspired by making your inner voice more positive about your pursuit.

Make an investment in improving the core types of intelligence that will enhance your ability to be creative when you are at work.

> *Creative individuals thrive when they are given all the freedom they need to solve a set of restrictive problems.*

15

When Don't
Matters More

● ● ● · · ● ● ●

"People are not perfect...very often
the relationships that are strongest
are those where people have worked
through big crises, but they've had to
work through them. So the challenge
to us is to work through that."

Patricia Hewitt

As you venture along life's journey, you will discover there are some people in the world that cross your path so you can learn who NOT to be.

Life is a mixture of good and bad, and if you are going to be a success, then you will need to observe and evolve from the negative lessons you learn from these unpleasant sorts.

Tough By Design: Job #15

By the time I started my 15th job, I was just graduating from The University of Nebraska – Lincoln and could not wait to find my dream job after college. After submitting my resume and applying to several hotel chains to be one of their hotel designers and several local jobs, I was offered two jobs at the same time. One offer was for The Marriott Hotels in Bethesda, MD, for $20,000 a year, and the other position was for a large local office and retail developer in Omaha, NE, for $17,000 a year. After much contemplation, I decided to stay at home and took a position with KV International, Inc as an in-house office interior designer. My boss was…well, he was a hard man. He was a short, unattractive man who carried a big stick.

I will just say that when I came back from going somewhere on lunch, I would find all of my work from the top of my desk on my chair. As I said, a tough man!

- A job is an eclectic place where you meet a lot of people. Chances are you are going to meet some "difficult" types that show you who you do not want to be.

- Seize the opportunity when it presents itself. If you work with a horrible person, take notes. Why do you not like them? What about them gets on your nerves? You can use these insights to evolve as a person into someone who is not like that.

- At my interior design job, I learned to be tougher. It was the most formal environment I had ever worked in, and there was rivalry and competition among the staff. I quickly learned what I would do to get ahead and what I would not do.

- This first position after college had a lot of responsibilities dealing with other large corporations that were expecting my expertise on my design capabilities. A lot of times I just had to portray I had years of experience, and I gained a lot of confidence with each project.

Stuck in Ruts and Circles

In the 1800s, when there were lots of horses and carts, a rut was the channel that would form in the dirt road when many carts and coaches wheeled by.

When one of these coaches became wedged in the rut and could only move a few inches forward and a few inches back, people would say it is "stuck in a rut." The saying has since caught on as a great way to describe the stagnancy that happens in a career.

I experienced this once later on in my career, and even though I went through it in my mind time and time again–going round in circles–I could not stand to see my days roll by with no progress.

- I left my job in the corporate world because I became tired. I would hear that Sugarland song on the radio, telling me "there has to be something more," and I knew that they were right. I was stuck in a rut.

- Working as hard as you can for the same salary with a meager chance at a raise once a year was not working out for me. I had places to go, people to meet. This job began weighing me down, so I left.

- I did not want to become the kind of person that sits at the same cubicle year after year, holding the same job title and the same salary. There might be some people that are okay with that, but I am not one of them.

- Once you have soaked up all the knowledge you can from a job, you should move on. There is no reason in this economy to stay in a position that is not fast-tracking you to a better quality of life. At the very least, it should teach you something innovative.

Confidence and Humble Pie

Confidence may be one of the most important factors in business success these days. Everybody goes through times when they do not feel prepared or good enough, but this is a feeling you need to learn to control early on.

Being self-conscious and unconfident are two features that will make colleagues and bosses immediately dismiss your value. No one wants to rely on someone who does not believe in themselves. The outcome will be negative before you have even begun!

This raised the question–how could I be confident without being cocky? I needed to learn how to strut my stuff while eating some humble pie.

- Confidence tells people what you can handle. When they are secure in the knowledge that you can handle something, they will be happy, and you will perform better. The opposite is true if you are visibly unconfident.

- The key to confidence is preparation. Practice always makes perfect, so if you are a little shy, practice being confident. Pretend until you feel able to do it truthfully. Prepare to be confident by pretending to be confident– the rest will come.

- Get feedback from people around you. Being self-aware means taking what people say about you to heart. If you are being a bit too controlling or arrogant, dial it down.

Likability has more power in business than useless traits like arrogance.

• Meet challenges head on. Never run away from a fight, even if you are hopelessly outmatched. The learning opportunity there is immense! Even if you fail, the experience will make you succeed the next time around. It is a win–win.

The more you do something, the better you will become at it. That is just common sense! Become a master at your job so that people come to you when they want something done right.

> *Be confident, but be humble–and you will be able to handle any situation that comes your way.*

Finding Out Who You Are

I did not know what I wanted to do; I only knew that I did not want to be stuck in the same job for the next 20 years.

It is hard to decide what to do with your life. Luckily, you do not actually have to do one thing–you can do several things, work in several niches, if that is what makes you happy.

• *Keep a daily journal.* When you are active in your personal development, it means you can benefit greatly from a journal filled with your goals and dreams. They also act as excellent motivators for when you do not feel inspired to push forward.

- *Learn to accept your strengths and weaknesses.* Try to identify them so that you can enhance your strengths and eliminate your weaknesses over time. It is hard to do, but ask a close family member or friend to give you honest feedback on both so you can learn from them and improve.

- *Be a bit selfish.* Sometimes it takes deep introspection to begin to understand who we are as people. You will need "me" time so that you can reflect on your day and plan to be better in the future. I would suggest working out with a friend, yoga, or meditation as they all de-stress, relax, and fortify you.

- *Use the "mirror theory" to identify traits in others that you do not like.* Write about them, and explore them in your own personality. Try to be the person you want to be, not the person who is saddled with negative behaviors.

Finding out who you are takes many years, but it helps if it is one of the goals that you have to work on day by day. With every job you do, you learn from the people who work there. Absorb the great traits from the people that impress you, and take note of the traits and habits that you do not want moving forward.

16

You're in the Biz, Baby

• • • • · · • •

"The first part of success is 'Get-to-it-iveness'; the second part of success is 'Stick-to-it-iveness.'"
Orison Swett Marden

Business is an exciting field when you apply it to a dynamic niche such as acting, movies, and television. I always wanted to be famous, so I followed one of my dreams to Hollywood.

Of all the jobs I had, this one had been the most interesting of all. Everything was fast-paced, explosive, and smothered in passion.

The Queen's Valet: Jobs #16&17

For jobs #16 and #17 I applied for an internship (I was a 31-year-old intern) at the University of California – Los Angeles to find out how actors got selected for their roles on television. I was accepted and went on to work as a casting assistant director for two of the top casting directors in the industry: two tough women–Vicki and Debra–both very different from each other in working styles.

It was extremely exciting to be around famous people and to work in such an exclusive career. Both casting directors were known for being very tough at auditions, but I learned a lot from both women.

- Everyone knew the casting director had a lot of power and was the boss selecting the actors to be on top television shows. The one casting director commanded an almost mythical respect from people, which was very impressive.

- The main thing I learned from both casting directors is they have an impeccable memory. If you auditioned once before and did terrible, they would remember that audition and never see you again. You must always be prepared, just like a Girl Scout!

- Being an intern is low on the totem pole, but it is a great way to break into a tough industry. You can learn a great deal from a top person in the industry and meet other people who have been in the industry for a long time.

- You are only as good as the next show. If you are not the top or the best, you can always be replaced by someone else. In this industry, any mistake will cost you your job, and it is the talk of the town. You must always be on your A+ game at all times and be looking for the next gig.

Under and Over: The Rules of the Game

My father spoke at length about his business strategy, so I felt that going into it in more detail would be beneficial for you. The rules of business dictate that you should stick to deadlines, be responsive, focus on customer care, always operate with integrity–that kind of thing.

But how do you manage the expectations of clients that want things yesterday?

By using the "under promise, over deliver" approach. And this is why.

- Customers like to know what is happening when they deal directly with a business. Businesses are even more insistent about knowing timelines and expectations. When you under promise, you set the bar low.

- Setting the bar low makes room for over delivery. If a client is expecting 10 crates of chicken on Thursday, send them 12 crates on Monday and blow their minds. This is how you create an air of expectation for your business that is manageable.

- Most people in business have terrible rules they follow when dealing with customers and other business affiliates. They over promise and under deliver. When you do this, you are telling your community that you cannot keep your promises.

- This could result in some clients breaking off and deciding to search for those crates of chicken elsewhere. Imagine being promised 10 crates of chicken on Thursday and only receiving five crates the following Tuesday. Not good for business.

Dominance and Servitude: A Lesson

Since I was released into the working world, I have tried to make it, even though men ruled the roost in every sense. These days it is easier for a woman to make it, though we face the same challenges as men and that glass ceiling nonsense has still not gone away.

This is why I believe that you need to learn an adequate lesson in dominance and servitude. I was lucky in that I purposefully kept up with the boys when I was a child.

- Men are naturally dominant. This is great for leadership, management, and big-picture thinking. Unfortunately, many men struggle with servitude. They do not lead by example; they dictate. You must not be this way.

- Women are naturally prone to servitude. We are great at working in teams, collaborating, and generally being good "employees." Unfortunately, we struggle with leadership, we do not take a hard enough line when managing, and we would rather allow problems to persist than deal with them.

- Yes, these are two VERY general observations. You will be different, I know that. But this is a common problem in business, as you will discover. The good news is if you focus, you can become a balanced leader who is great at correctly enforcing business rules and practices.

- Do not be too dominant, and do not be too servile.

You need a good balance. Lead by DOING. Do not be afraid to ask for opinions and help. You never know enough to be beyond reproach. Things change all the time–change with them! A good leader is someone that is at the front of the line when their troops march into battle. A bad one dictates from behind the lines.

Overrated Talent and Business

Another key lesson I want to stress to you is this. No one owes you anything. You might be extraordinarily talented, but unless you can convert that talent into income for the business, you should not feel like you are better than other employees around you.

Of course, if you bring in a million bucks for your company, then fine, talk about your superior talent in the office. Until then, be humble. Humility is not a weakness in business; it is a strength, and it is one of the most likable traits in a leader.

- Do not overrate your talent at work or in public. Unless you have proven your worth, it comes across as mindless boasting.

- Never announce that you can do something that you cannot do. You never know when someone might check up on that.

- You are a human asset. But it is not the company's job to increase your value; it is your job. If you want to earn more, SHOW the bosses your incredible talent.

- Most success comes from 5% talent and 95% hard work. I would suggest proving your worth by adding in some extra hours with a very definite result.

- If you find yourself unable to work extremely hard, then try working smart. Organize your work properly, schedule your time effectively, and come up with a strategy to get noticed in your company.

Playing It Fast and Loose

The two casting director women showed me how Hollywood operated, and I will always be grateful for that experience.

Originally the phrase fast and loose was based on a game where something appeared to be stuck fast, but it was actually loose–so there was some cheating involved. These days the term has evolved to mean risky.

- Vicki was a risk taker. She demanded respect from the people around her, and they willingly supplied her with that respect.

- You cannot run a successful business these days without taking calculated risks. As long as you can control the PR of your business, any mistakes that are made can remain separate from the company name.

- A good business owner knows how to take risks, be vulnerable, and learn from their mistakes. By keeping the brand solid and separate from the owner, the owner is able to make those mistakes, be flexible, and continue to learn in a rigid environment.

- You will not be able to discover new opportunities and innovation if you do not learn to take risks. Do it in your life and in business. There is nothing worse than someone who is unwilling to break out of their comfort zone.

No one remembers how brilliant innovations and ideas come about, only that they did and they were successful. The risks an individual took are never recalled, so do not be afraid to do a little fast and loose business yourself.

Manage and control RISK appropriately and you will become a business superstar.

17

Follow the Yellow Brick Road

● ● ● · · ● ●

"Learning is the beginning of
wealth. Learning is the beginning of
health. Learning is the beginning of
spirituality. Searching and learning is
where the miracle process all begins."
Jim Rohn

M oney makes the world go around. It is also the reason why you get to sleep, eat, and venture out of your home in comfort. Without money, your world stops.

That is why you have to follow the yellow brick road. Just like Dorothy in *The Wizard of Oz* (one of my favorite movies of all time), we are all just moving down life's path towards a brighter future at home.

My mother always used to say that patience comes to those who wait. It is a variation of the popular saying "good things come to those who wait," only it makes far more sense.

In life and in business, it is important to practice patience daily. Although your mind is brimming with ideas, the world moves at its own sturdy pace.

When the Earth Shakes: Job #18

Around job number #17, I was very content in my life until one morning at 4:31 a.m. Pacific time on January 17, 1994, when the 6.7 magnitude earthquake occurred in Northridge, CA, about 18 miles from where I was living at the time in Burbank, CA. So for job #18, a company called me the next day to hire me as a consultant to work with all of the retailers on repairing the damage to a shopping center that had experienced some major earthquake damage. My job was to assist in assessing the damage to their stores and how long it would take to reopen.

I was hired for seven months, and the money was well worth it. Unfortunately, it had unwanted side effects. Being so close to a shopping center redirected my life back there–to retail world. I regret that looking back, but I know where I went wrong.

- Do not follow the money, because it will lead you astray. I should have followed my passion instead, but the earthquake shopping center cash was just too good.

- When you do something completely for the safety risk, expect consequences. I became concerned for my safety during each aftershock at the mall and wondered if the building was going to come crashing on my head. Money cannot be worth it if your life may be in danger.

- At this stage of my life, all I wanted was security from money. Instead, I managed to find myself working in a disaster-orientated field that could have environmental risks to my health. Now that was an experience to remember.

A Temporary Solution: Jobs #19, 20, 21

Jobs #19, #20, and #21 were all related to working for three different shopping center owners. I preferred consulting work because I did not have to get tied into an employment contract, and I could leave at any time.

- After the mall reopened, the company decided to bring me on full time, and they moved to Dallas in 1996, which co-incidentally is a great place to raise a family and start a business.

- After working for the large retail/office/industrial developer for a few years as an employee, they decided to sell their U.S. company, and everyone was out of a job. The positive was I was paid a excellent, one–year severance package, and the company that bought their retail portfolio hired me as a consultant for another year.

- Finally, I took my last temp job as a consultant and tenant coordinator for a very large shopping center owner. It was a wonderful position and an ideal job as I had just had my first child. The offices were in the mall; I would bring along the baby stroller and work in quiet bliss. I still laugh about bringing my baby to work and not caring since I was a consultant, and if they did not like it, I would just quit. They did not mind at all.

Waiting for Your Moment

I have always struggled with patience since childhood. I was always the one running around, trying new things, and getting into a little trouble.

When it comes to practicing patience in your life, you need to be realistic. Success does not happen in an instant. It is a gradual process. The same can be said for eventually owning your own business.

- See every job opportunity as a learning curve and as an addition to your store of business knowledge. Even if you do not know what you want to do with your life just yet, I promise you that any job will offer you some key lessons.

- You will have a moment one day where a great idea pops into your mind. You will not be able to stop thinking about it. Excitement will rise, and then you will be able to plan and set up your first business. When this happens, it will be an indispensable asset if you have been actively learning about business this entire time.

Patience is difficult to apply when you are talking about a lifetime's worth of it. But begin small by being patient in day-to-day life. You will need to learn this skill if you are going to become an effective CEO.

A Step or Two in the Right Direction

There are many ways you can learn to manage or improve how patient you are. Believe me, in your first direct conflict in a business meeting, you will need this skill.

By taking a gentle step or two in the right direction, you can learn to effectively manage your impatience using some of these easy techniques:

- Practice empathetic listening and active listening. Give people your full attention when they speak to you. Do not think about how what they are saying is going to affect you. Listen to how it is affecting them.

- Always nurture the ability to laugh at yourself. If you have become so impatient that you do something silly, who cares–laugh about it! Everyone becomes overwhelmed and frustrated sometimes. It is how you react to it that matters.

Taking these small steps in the right direction will keep you moving towards becoming a balanced leader in business. This is what you should be reaching for.

I also learned taking on a few consulting and temporary jobs would give me the flexibility to leave on my own terms. This gives a great sense of power to control your own life goals.

18

Give a Little to Get a Lot

● ● ● · · ● ● ●

"Authority is not a quality one person 'has,' in the sense that he has property or physical qualities. Authority refers to an interpersonal relation in which one person looks upon another as somebody superior to him."

Erich Fromm

After my first child and all those temp jobs, I was feeling the need for a proper career. In order to achieve that, I needed to learn about authority, and I did that at my next position.

Being a person who is considered an authority figure is not just a compliment. It is a way for community members to identify you as a leader and as someone they can trust.

It Is Who You Know: Job #22

My #22 job was a really good one. I was hired on as a Property Development Manager at Brinker International, Inc., which is one of the largest casual dining restaurant companies with more than 1,500 restaurants in the world. I can truly say that out of all of my previous jobs, I learned the most about business from this one.

I was hired without any real experience in developing restaurants at all. I got the job purely because I knew someone, and she asked me if I would like to come on board as part of the team.

> *Business is very much about WHO you know, not what you know. You cannot be a success in business if you do not know the right people. Key people make businesses grow.*

After coming back to work after being a stay at home mom for a few years, I was tossed into a very fast-paced environment. I thought everyone was talking 100 miles an hour and I would NEVER catch on. It took only a short three months before I was finally running at the same speed as my team.

Working at Brinker taught me a great deal about having a culture about your company. If you did not fit the "culture" of the company, you would NEVER be hired with them. The culture was fun, casual, but you worked hard.

> *Keeping an open mind in business is one of the hardest things to do, especially once you have attained success. Your employees are a total asset, and they will keep you processing new ideas if you let them.*

Asking the Right Kind of Questions

Being open to personal growth is a vastly understated skill for business owners and executives these days. The whole point of gaining authority is to be a better leader–for yourself and your employees.

That is why questions are the answer for the up and coming business owner or leader. Every day there are new problems that need to be solved. Businesses fail because these problems are never adequately addressed and all because of nonsense reasons—like ego or the inability to ask for help from your team.

- If you are going to give a little to get a lot in return, you must be prepared to learn. There is always something new to learn from the people around you, and you should realize that different perspectives fit like puzzle pieces to make the brightest, most attractive pictures.

- You know and understand a lot, but you will never reach the point where this is enough. It is difficult to know what to do when pressed for decisions and solutions as a business leader. Become comfortable with not having all the answers, and seek out help. Authority grows when you have the humility to find the best answer.

- When you trust the people around you enough to make them a part of your business decisions, it radically improves relationships within your company. Plus it proves to your employees that you are open-minded, curious, and always searching for the "best" instead of settling on past experiences to guide current actions.

Being a Superior Leader

One of my favorite stories about leadership involves two tribal chiefs vying over the same strip of land. Both chiefs were known for their skill in battle and their clever tactical moves when outflanking and overwhelming invading forces. The first chief was a practical man and preferred to lead the charge in battle. The second chief was more of a thinker and always remained in a safe spot while sending commands to his warriors.

When they eventually faced each other on the field of battle, only one chief could win. While both were famed for their leadership ability, at the end it came down to who had won the most respect from their warriors. The practical chief who was always at the front, experiencing what his warriors experienced, was uniquely in tune with the skill of every man. He won the land because he was the superior leader.

Earning authority in business is very much the same. "Bosses" forget that it is solid relationships, practical experience, and "togetherness" that leads to employee loyalty and respect. You cannot win authority if your employees believe you lead from a golden pedestal. Like the first chief, you must earn respect through engagement so that when the time comes, you will not only behave like a leader but your employees will naturally look to you for practical guidance. That is real authority.

19

It's Secret,
It's Saucy

• • • • • • •

"Hold yourself responsible for a higher standard than anyone else expects of you. Never excuse yourself."

Henry Ward Beecher

Ihave always wondered why they do not teach self-improvement in schools. It is the single most worthwhile pursuit that is meant to last a lifetime.

If you do love working on yourself mentally, spiritually, and physically, then you have to hide it away like it is some kind of bad new age secret. Well, the secret is out! And it is saucy.

Bouncing Back and Forth: Jobs #23&24

By the time job #22 was winding down, I decided to start my very own real estate company. Goodwin Commercial Properties was born in 2006 as job #23. By Job #24, I thought I needed to go back to joining another real estate company to be part of a larger team (this only lasted one year before I realized it was not true).

I began the business with a partner who had been in the business more than 50 years, and it was a high-impact learning process that nothing can really prepare you for. It was a fantastic break from the slog of the 9–5 life, and new possibilities shone saucily on the horizon. I wanted them. I wanted them all!

It was the first time in my career that I looked forward to my Mondays, even though I was now working seven-day weeks. I can honestly say that the thrill of starting your own business does not compare to anything else. You get to make your own decisions, and you are responsible for everything–both good and bad. What makes it so exciting is the learning lessons along the way.

- When you finally feel ready to start your own business, do so. Take all the lessons you learned from your other jobs and compile a business journal.

- You will know when you are ready because you will feel empowered. Jot down all your ideas, prepare your business plan, do everything by the book, and get your network team started!

Everything Happens for a Reason

I am a firm believer that everything happens for a good reason. Whether positive or negative, you learn things based on the experiences that you have to live through.

In business, even though you have no experience (or limited experience), I would suggest opening your mind to different possibilities and looking around for a complementary partner.

- *Sort out the admin side of your business.* You will only be able to grow as a business owner if you do not have to constantly fix the mistakes you made when you began to set up the business.

- *Taxes, forms, licenses, and contracts are critical.* If you need any of these, make sure they are done by a lawyer who works for you and has your best interests in mind. If another lawyer revamps a contract, have yours look it over again.

- *Choose a business partner who will work well with you.* Do not go into business with a friend. Select someone who has the specific skill sets that you need. If they cannot bring anything valuable to the table, they are NOT a good choice.

- Watch the people around you closely, and form systems. When your business first starts functioning, notice how your team works. Correct lazy behaviors and inefficient practices. Everything should be a test in efficiency.

- *Work on yourself.* You will be reviewing your own personal journey and adding to it as you progress. Self-development is key to growing along with your business from the grass roots stages.

If you make a mistake in business, see it as a learning curve. Pick yourself up, dust yourself off, and keep your team motivated. Never give up. And never allow the hopeless attitudes of others to infect you or your team.

Cool by Association

I have experienced what real authority and presence feels like.

- In June 1974 I went to an Elvis Presley concert in Omaha. My mom was able to score front row seats to see him, and my mom brought us kids along to experience the King of Rock and Roll. I was only 10 at the time and remember the concert like it was yesterday. I brought with me one of my dad's white handkerchiefs and walked up to Elvis while he was singing and handed it to him. Elvis slid his dark blue silk scarf off his sweaty neck in return, and I screamed with joy. I still have the scarf hidden away in a very secure location.

- I have never forgotten the power of his presence. He had the crowd under his entire spell. It was a show to never be forgotten. I saw him once more before his death in 1977.

*Elvis Presley first row ticket stub for concert
I attended on June 30, 1974*

- I was also fortunate enough to meet several celebrities while working at my casting jobs. I happened to be at a house party when I met Barbra Streisand–and I was such a big fan that the excitement nearly killed me!

- These encounters each taught me a little more about presence and authority. Elvis and Barbra were the voices of our generation. They had style, class, and personality–and people loved their music.

- At this stage, I had already discovered that communities would play an important role in my business in the future. If a fan base can rally around stars such as Elvis and Barbra, then why not around leaders in their community?

Books and Balances

Self-improvement at work begins with the very first choices that you will make for your business. One of those crucial choices involves the finance of your company.

Choosing an excellent accountant to do your books is exactly what you need from day one. Do not get your cousin to do your books because it is cheaper. This is a business, not some small-time operation with no growth potential.

- Understand what an accountant does, and find one with clear evidence of success. A poor accountant is not a particularly good one.

- The same can be said for your financial advisor. Always have more than one; the optimal number is four. Then you can check their advice against the others and decide based on your own research and four streams of expert advice.

- Getting off to a good start means hunting for a system that works for your company. If you send the books through every Thursday, then set that as a rule. It will help you manage your time, and you will prevent overloading your accountant with work after a few months.

- Always make sure your books and balances are in order. I think of my books as the body of my business. If they are not healthy, then my business is not healthy and things need to change. Know how much money you are bringing in, spending, and using on a day-to-day basis, and tighten the purse strings. Think of how many celebrities have ended up broke because they hired the wrong person to manage their money.

- You need to take an active role in delegating this work and OVERSEEING it. You cannot simply hand over information and expect it to work out. Managing your own finances is a set rule. Do not leave it to a stranger who does not care.

Breaking (ALL) the Rules

Once you fully understand the rules of self-improvement and business development–break them. Break ALL of them. That is what they are they for. But be cautious–only an expert that is well-orientated in a niche can break the rules with success and begin to see opportunity where others only see blank space.

- *Work on your schedule.* A schedule is not something you sit down and create; it is a work in progress–something to be perfected by you. The tighter your schedule, the more work you can fit in a day and the more income you will bring in.

- *Infuse yourself into your business.* If you are quite a fun-loving person, then make your business fun. It may seem unconventional, but many people appreciate it. Remember your client base is made up of normal people.

- *Adopt an attitude of generosity and gratitude.* Business owners are often told to be selfish and stingy with their money. While that is common practice, you can achieve a lot more in a community if you are generous and gracious. This is how I got my network together, and I still make money through them every day.

- *Do you have anything in your life or business holding you back?* You will find as a business owner that your identity becomes chained to your business. Make sure there is nothing in your life or in your business that is keeping you from moving forward. Break free of those chains, and surge ahead.

Never stop trying new things. Every time I go online to conduct research, I find out something new about marketing or a marketing process. Do not be afraid to try new things to discover how best to do business.

The Story of Self-Reliance

Being someone who values self-improvement will convert you into a reader for life. Books have an amazing power to teach you things that you really need to know, even though you did not realize you needed to know them!

I have always been very self-reliant. Even though I was brought up to live the conventional life of "husband, kids, career," I have always been driven to earn for myself. I want my own set of successes in this life; I do not want to have to rely on anyone else for income.

- *Do not rely on anyone else to support you.* This applies to business but also to life in general. It is not all right to spend your life beholden to someone else's finances. If they leave, what have you got? Nothing.

- *You have the ability to be completely self-reliant.* You have been given gifts and talents that you can develop into serious assets for your company.

- *When you rely on others to support you, it makes for endless arguments, unnecessary tension, and conflict in otherwise good relationships.* People do not like to give other people their hard-earned money, even if that person is their spouse.

- *Supporting yourself means that you will need to come up with the cash to start your company.* Do not borrow money from an individual. It is better to have cash. Cash is king!

Let me tell you a quick story about self-reliance. When you expect to be given an apple every day for nothing, you begin to count on it. And life is notoriously unreliable. One day that apple could vanish with all the other apples. Panic will set in. You should perfect your own formula for getting yourself those apples every day!

20

The Research Raven

• • • • • • •

"Research is to see what everybody else has seen, and to think what nobody else has thought."

Albert Szent-Gyorgyi

I have been researching everything since I realized the Internet was a doorway into all the collected knowledge of the world.

Because of this, I have become known as the "research queen," and I often have clients, friends, and family coming to me for my excellent online research abilities.

The Reality State: Job #25

My current job–job number #25–was my dream job. After all of those positions, people, and experiences, I finally found the skills I needed to become successful on my own once again. After more than 25 years of my career, it comes down to it that the best position by far is working for yourself.

My first development project on my own with my business partner was acquiring and assembling two parcels for a combination of five acres in Tyler, TX. With the relationships, I had developed the three top tenants in their categories: a Walgreens, a Chase Bank, and a McDonald's. I would have never had the confidence to pull this project off without the experience I had gained throughout the years. I had developed more than 50 new restaurant sites for Chili's and On the Border concepts throughout the U.S.

Armed with the knowledge I had painstakingly learned over the years and a whole new world of knowledge on the Internet, things became easier.

- Learn how to research properly and thoroughly online. I am not talking about a Google page one search. Even if you only use top search results, it means your keyword usage needs to be good.

- If you ever have a question, are wondering about a new marketing technique, or need a case study to back up your suspicions, it is very likely online already. All you have to do is reach out and comb through some bad information until you reach the good stuff.

- Research online is like having access to the CIA and KGB databases 40 years ago. The amount of power that you have is insurmountable, though it is downplayed today in a modern context because of information overload.

When I finally returned to my own company, I knew that this time I would succeed. In just a few short years of applying the lessons I learned in this book, I became a very successful and highly regarded person in my industry. Now I focus on wealth generation and doing the job I love so much.

You Will Like This Kind of Math

We all attend the "school of hard knocks"–that is what life is all about. But whether you graduate from this school or drop out is completely up to you. Students of life that work hard, learn, study, experience, and take risks are the ones that get all the rewards.

It takes a lifetime to realize that the real assets in your life are the people around you. Getting started is so much easier when you have people to help you do it.

- Most people ask me, how did you become successful? My answer is the same every time–because of other people! You will like this kind of math. It involves starting a referral program so that everyone can make money.

- I use referral marketing to maximize community sales potential in the real estate industry. That means I inform, encourage, promote, and reward my clients as much as possible. They basically do the work for me.

- Everyone knows someone who owns real estate or is looking to buy their first piece of real estate. When you work in a close-knit community, your network will bring you those customers primed and ready to buy.

- While this is not the right sales formula for everyone (it works like magic in real estate), it is indicative of the many hundreds of ways that you could turn a small business into a thriving corporation if you wanted to.

- Research helped me iron out the kinks in my referral marketing plans. It helped me find people, set up meetings, maintain contact, make new connections, and advance the sale of my properties. The Internet is one of your greatest assets, second only to your mind.

When you have spent a few years learning all you can about your chosen industry, you will be ready to strike out on your own–like I did–to secure your success. When you know what to do, success happens in just a few short years after that. The time investment is not only worth it–it is math that anyone can make sense of.

> *Nurture a passion for cash flow, and you will quickly discover how powerful your business can become in a short time if you save, store, and reinvest for growth.*

Time Kills Deals

I have learned a lot from my time working in the commercial real estate industry. It is a wonderfully complex and multi-faceted niche that always has something new to learn.

If there is one dominant thing that I learned, it is that time kills deals. You have to be so on the mark when negotiating a commercial property deal that it becomes a thrilling process. Wait too long, and the buyer will move on to another place.

- Always make friends with a city approvals expert so that you can get great advice and run all of your needs directly through them. This is how you save time and get the right approvals done when you need them.

- Hire the right consultants. You will need to have a staff of experts on your side to help you navigate the heavily moderated development industry. Find great property managers, developers, engineers, architects, and agents–have them all in your network.

- When you have the right network of people to help you buy, build, and sell, it makes your job a lot easier. In fact, with a top team, you can make significantly more than other real estate developers based on the advice you are given and can discover via research online.

- Think of the Internet as your unofficial business partner. Check everything there to try and keep yourself away from common mistakes and working towards the greatest likelihood of success.

Once again–time kills. In business, this is true even outside of real estate. You need people and the ability to research when you run into problems so that you can solve them fast. This is how you can push deals through in record time.

Your ABCs: Life by Design

We are all in charge of our own lives. At some point everyone realizes this and freaks out. But when you live life by design–with

purpose and clear goals–there is nothing you cannot achieve. I am not just saying that; I have lived it. I have taught it.

That is why you need to get your ABCs in order. Learn the basics. Then spend a good few years focused on the more advanced, practical side of your training. If it is all part of your life plan, then you will not mind going to work each day. There is purpose there.

- My philosophy on life is the ABC method. **A**lways **B**e **C**losing! I did not become a successful real estate guru by wasting my time and staying in jobs that I did not like. Always Be Closing is a great philosophy; it means that you are constantly in pursuit of the next big success achievement.

- I only ever take on deals that have a 50/50 chance of paying off. Everything else is not important. I want to know that my time investment is going to pay off. I work less; I earn far more.

- Whenever I see businesses or land for sale, I consider the two big elements of my strategy: timing and price. If those two details are in the ideal acceptable areas, then my profit is all but guaranteed.

How far are you on your life journey? I am sure I have given you a lot to think about. There are lessons in this book that took serious time to learn, but hopefully you will learn them now before you strike out on your own.

Life Hacks I Have Learned along the Way

I have spent many years learning about multiple businesses, and I have stores of knowledge that would make an MBA professor blush.

Here are some life hacks I have learned along my personal journey to success. These are things that take years to learn, so study them carefully, and reap all the benefits.

1. Keep learning and growing every day.

2. Ask for the order.

3. Touch your customers every day or someone else will.

4. Today is a brand new day.

5. Pick up the phone.

6. Time is money.

7. Do not worry about stuff you cannot control.

8. Sale the sizzle.

9. You only have two things–Time and Information–so do not give either of them away

10. Be the go-to person.

11. Know when to move on.

12. Persistence pays off.

13. Be your own boss.

14. Clients' expectations.

15. Ask the right questions.

16. Take action, and follow through.

17. The best client is a repeat client.

18. Be unique and memorable.

19. Do not put it off–do it today.

20. Never, Never, Never give up.

21. Fortune is in the follow-up.

22. Respond is positive; react is negative.

23. Keep trying; it will pay off if you want it bad enough.

24. Time pressure makes us act without thinking for the fear of losing out.

25. Have fun!

If you are not willing to listen in business, then do not expect to learn anything new. Everyone has something that is worth sharing and learning.

The real difference between success and failure is persistence. If you give up, you fail. But it is impossible to fail when you refuse to give up.

Once you give people the answer they have been looking for, they stop listening to you. Leave clues instead, and make them want more.

> *The more you "fail," the closer you will get to succeeding. If you are not failing, then you are not shooting for success.*

CONCLUSION

I spent a lifetime working in 25 different jobs, and you know what I learned?

Life is short, and time flies by at the speed of light. If you want to spend at least some of your time here relaxing, enjoying yourself, and basking in your success, then you have to start now.

There is nothing wrong with switching your job dozens of times. It is rare that people know what they want to do when they are in their early 20s. The key here is that you have a life strategy, an overall goal to absorb what you can and use it on your own success journey.

At every job, I learned something more about myself–who I am, what I believe in, what I do not tolerate. You have to get out there and DO if you want to figure out which job is the right one for you. No one will help you do that but yourself.

With so much choice in today's world, you do not want information overload to turn into "life overload." Yes, it is easy sitting in front of the TV, playing games, and working at your boring 9–5 to get that hallowed paycheck every month.

But think ahead. You will need money when you are older. You will need security and support, and that all comes from your bank account. I managed to take everything that I learned in business and produced something valuable from it.

Take my advice, and learn these lessons now. You do not want to live a life of regret when you get older. And even if you are a little older, it is never too late to claim the success that life can offer you. All you have to do is develop yourself as an asset–the best you will ever have.

Be your best!

Pamela Goodwin

Made in the USA
Middletown, DE
18 July 2015